速寫建築：

一九四九年以來的中國建築寫作與創建

WRITING IN(TO) ARCHITECTURE:

Chinaʼs Architectural Design and Construction Since 1949

出版　　**東坡出版有限公司**
Published by East Slope Publishing Limited

平面設計排版 Designer	楚 翹 Devorah Jowie Chan
印刷 Printer	思捷概念 CD Concept
版次 Edition	2012年8月初版 1st edition, August 2012
書號/ISBN:	978-988-15005-8-8
定價/Retail Price	港幣HK$120

Muse is a registered trademark of

East Slope Publishing Limited
Post Office Box 33744
Sheung Wan, Hong Kong

tel: +852 9170 5484
fax: +852 2541 1527
website: www.musemag.hk
email: muse@musemag.hk

Writing In(to) Architecture: China's Architectural Design and Construction Since 1949
速寫建築：一九四九年以來的中國建築寫作與創建

=================================
We have been unable to locate the sources/copyright holders for some of the images used in this book. If notified by the copyright holder, we should be pleased to append the appropriate acknowledgements or remove those images, if required to do so, in subsequent printings of the book.

本書部分圖片來源及版權未明，但若我方收到任何有關圖片來源及版權的通知，我方將樂意在隨後版次加上正確的圖片出處說明，或（在被要求的情況下）刪除圖片。

contents

1949-1978

GOVERNMENT PROPAGANDA: WRITING TO MANIPULATE

INTRODUCTORY ARTICLES: WRITING TO "INFORM"

COMMENTARIES: THE GOVERNMENT'S ONE-SIDED DEBATE

After 1978

INTRODUCTORY ARTICLES: RE-EMERGENCE OF THE INDIVIDUAL ARCHITECT

COMMENTARIES: EMERGENCE OF DIFFERENT OPINIONS IN THE POST-MAO ERA

目錄

acknowledgements

I owe my special thanks to Frank Proctor, as my English editor for his advice on the manuscript; as my publisher for making this book possible; and as my mentor for his always heart-warming encouragement and guidance.

I thank my Chinese editor Gloria Chow and art director Jowie Chan for making this book precise and for taking it far beyond mere text.

I thank Professor Marina Lathouri for her guidance on my thesis, and her assurance that architectural journalism in China is a topic worth working on, at a time when I had doubts about whether I had chosen the right direction to explore. I also wish to thank Professor Gene Mustain for his inspiration.

Finally, I thank my family for giving me the space, over the years, to read, to write, and to think. Their endless support, even at times when my ideas become too grotesque or my temper too unbearable, enables me to keep dreaming.

謝　辭

我特別希望感謝方博德先生 (Mr. Frank Proctor)，他是我的英文編輯，就本書的文本給了很多意見；他是我的山版人，令此書山版得以成真；他也足我的導師， 直鼓勵及指導著我。

感謝我的中文編輯周允寧女士及藝術總監陳楚翹女士，她們確保本書精確，並在文字以外，豐富了本書的內涵。

感謝 Marina Lathouri 教授指導我的論文，並在我懷疑所研究的題目是否適合時，令我確信中國建築傳媒是值得探討的課題。我亦希望感謝麥銳哲教授 (Professor Gene Mustain) 的啟發。

最後，我希望感謝家人這些年來給予我閱讀、寫作及思考的空間。儘管有時我萌生非常奇怪的念頭，又或暴躁難耐，他們仍不斷支持我，令我得以繼續追尋夢想。

who builds

An artist is just a medium. Meaning is also created by viewers and audiences.

- Marcel Duchamp

In an ArchNewsNow.com interview published in September 2011, architect Daniel Libeskind recalls his close to ten years' involvement in redeveloping the World Trade Center complex, where the National 9/11 Memorial (*Reflecting Absence*), the first major element of the complex, was finally completed a decade after the terrorist attack. Other parts of the complex are still under construction. Describing the endless rounds of revisions and even redesigns of his master plan, which had been selected from among more than 2,000 proposals submitted to New York's Innovative Design Contest, Libeskind says: "Architecture changed fundamentally. Now, not only in New York and America, but just about everywhere, you no longer can build even small projects without public participation. People now want to know what is being built. Why is it this way? What is the meaning of this and that? Who is building it? Is it sustainable? ...It is no longer satisfactory to rely on decisions made in closed corporate boardrooms. The public now wants to participate in the process of building our environment."[1]

Recent projects around the world exemplify the more prominent role that public participation plays in architecture. Superkilen in Copenhagen, designed by the Danish architectural firm BIG and completed in 2011, positions itself as an open art work composed of diverse objects chosen by citizens, "which will gain content and take form in a dialogue with the users and citizens of the area."[2] Hong Kong's West Kowloon Cultural District project underwent three rounds of public engagement exercises in 2011 concerning the design brief, the master plan, and the detailed development plan before the cornerstone could finally be laid. Architecture has traditionally been a field in which professional architects claimed to have the exclusive knowledge essential for design. The weight given to public participation in these recent projects, however, would seem to suggest otherwise: that the public not only have the right, but also the ability, to participate in architectural discussions and contribute to the design of their immediate surroundings.

The general public could have been given a larger role in architectural design long before now. Architecture is not an autonomous art form for the individual pursuit of aesthetics, but is the key component of the cityscape, and is thus instrumental for our engagement in society. Architects do not work for themselves, but must respond to social, economic, cultural and political issues. Ultimately, they have a responsibility to respond to the needs

1   http://www.archnewsnow.com/features/Feature369.htm

2   http://www.big.dk/projects/suk/

為誰而建

藝術家只是一種媒介。意義同時由觀者與聽眾創造。

── 馬塞爾・杜象

在2011年9月ArchNewsNow.com出版的一篇訪問中，建築師丹尼爾・李伯斯金(Daniel Libeskind)憶述了他參與世貿中心樓群重建的近十年經歷；在恐怖襲擊十年後，樓群的首個主要部分 ── 911紀念堂「反映逝者」終於落成，而樓群其他部分仍然在興建當中。李伯斯金回想起其於2003年由超過2,000份建案中脫穎而出、勝出紐約創意設計大賽的規劃藍圖，經歷了無數次的修改甚至重新設計，他說：「建築徹底改變了。現在，不單在紐約及美國，而是在幾乎每個角落，你已經不可以在不牽涉公眾參與下建設項目，甚至是小項目。大眾現在希望知道你在興建甚麼。為甚麼是這個樣子呢？這些東西的意思是甚麼？是誰在興建？是可持續的嗎？……單靠在閉門的企業會議室裡所作的決定已不足夠。大眾現在希望知道怎樣參與建設共同的環境。」[1]

世界各地近期的項目亦顯示出公眾參與在建築領域中日益重要 ── 由丹麥建築事務所 BIG 設計、2011年建成、位於哥本哈根的 Superkilen 公園項目，被定位成公共藝術，由當地市民選擇的多元化物件所構成，「透過跟使用者和當地市民對話，得到內涵及形象」；[2]香港的西九文化區自2011年經歷了三輪有關設計大綱、規劃藍圖及詳細發展計劃的討論，才終於可以動工興建。傳統上，在建築領域中，建築師應該擁有設計所必須的專門知識，但於近期項目中，公眾參與的比重似乎顯示這個情況已經改變：一般大眾不單有權利，而且有能力參與有關建築的討論，並為其身處環境的設計作出貢獻。

一般大眾本應在一早以前，就更廣泛參與建築設計。建築不是讓個人成就美學成果的自主藝術，而是城市的主要部分，因而是大眾參與社會事務的工具之一。建築師並非為自身工作，卻要面對社會、經濟、文化及政治議題。最終，他們有責任向空間使用者的需要負責。建成一個項目的過程牽涉多個界別 ── 發展商、投資者、政客、工程師、承建商及一般大眾。本書紀錄了自中華人民共和國成立以來，中國執業建築師的角色及地位改變，正如本書例子顯示，在任何時代或政治氣候下，建築師的工作都是找出一個可以滿足所有人士的設計方案。他們分配

1　http://www.archnewsnow.com/features/Feature369.htm

2　http://www.big.dk/projects/suk/

前言

of the users of a space. The process of realizing a piece of architecture involves various parties – developers, investors, politicians, engineers, contractors, and the public at large. As exemplified in this book, which charts the changing role and status of architects practicing in China since 1949, the job of an architect, in any era or political circumstances, is to find balanced design solutions that satisfy literally everyone. The architect channels construction resources and adds value to a space which otherwise would simply be inhabited and defined by its occupants. The long, complex process renders a piece of architecture not merely an object, but "a story about lives," to use Libeskind's term.

Architects only get involved once a decision to build has been made. In this sense, architects have the passive role of responding to the requirements of clients who commission them, rather than the active role of pursuing their individual creative visions, as artists do. Paradoxically, however, the commission of a project immediately transposes the power to make ultimate decisions about spatial design from client to architect. It sets the architect free. The architect takes on the role of "thinker" and "expert," becoming the authority who monopolizes the architectural discourse with the language of the discipline. Of course, different parties still give requirements or opinions about the design of a space, but it is the architect who translates these opinions into architectural language, which is often incomprehensible to laymen. The architect experiments with form, structure, the positioning in a certain context, etc., as if architecture were an autonomous discipline. When a design is completed, the architect explains how and why opinions from certain parties were incorporated, while others were not. Laymen, insufficiently eloquent in architectural language to respond, have no choice but to entrust the spatial design to the architect. Only the architect can verify whether certain opinions have informed the architectural design. The architect has the privilege of realizing architecture that in fact results from experimentation in an autonomous discipline, all in the name of responding to the needs of the occupants. *Writing In(to) Architecture* examines the ways architects in China tried to realize their architectural visions even in times of political turmoil, and their attempts to convince the general public that they built for the common good.

Only opinions formulated after rational-critical debates, backed up by architectural knowledge, can inform architectural design. Realizing that the general public have no specific training in architecture and can hardly engage in such debates, architects still feel an urge to recognize the importance of public participation in architecture. Architects assure the general public that their opinions are valued, though these opinions might be uninformed and could hardly inspire architectural design. Such a hypocritical position could be interpreted as originating from a kind of guilt: while the production of a painting involves only a blank canvas and paint, architectural production involves far more resources, most of which are not owned by the architect. A piece of architecture, unlike a painting in an artist's studio, can also significantly affect the context in which it is situated. The emphasis on personal creativity in architecture has a weaker moral standing, and is less "politically correct," than an emphasis on public participation. Even architects themselves do not seem

建築所需的資源，並為本來可以僅由使用者佔據及定義的空間增值。完成一個建築項目所需的漫長過程令建築成為不單一件物件，而是如李伯斯金所述的那種「有關生活的故事」。

　　建築師在作出興建項目的決定後才開始參與過程。在此層面上，建築師角色被動，只需回應委託他們的業主的要求，而非像藝術家一樣，可以主動地成就他們的設計願景。不過弔詭地，設計項目的委託立即造成一種權力轉移 ── 為空間設計作最終決定的權力由業主轉移到建築師身上。建築師得到了自由。他們擔當「思想家」及「專家」的角色，成為以專業語言壟斷建築論述的權威。當然，不同界別仍可就空間設計提出要求或意見，但建築師仍然負責將有關要求或意見翻譯成建築語言，而一般人往往無法明白建築語言。建築師就建築的外形、結構、與環境脈絡的關係等進行實驗，令建築成為一個似乎自主的專業。當一個設計建成後，建築師負責解釋某些界別的意見如何或怎樣被融合至設計當中，而為甚麼其他意見被否決。非界別的普羅大眾由於欠缺建築語言作出回應，於是唯有在無選擇的情況下相信建築師，讓他們設計空間。建築師成為可以證實某些意見是否影響了建築設計的唯一人選。他們擁有以滿足使用者需要之名，實際在其自主的界別進行試驗，創造建築的特權。《速寫建築》指出中國的建築師如何在政治動盪的環境下，仍然嘗試達成他們的建築願景，以及他們如何嘗試說服大眾他們是為了大眾幸福而建設。

　　只有在理智及具批判性討論下產生、並以建築知識為基礎的意見，才可以啟發建築設計。儘管建築師知道未受建築教育的大眾不大可能參與有關討論，建築師仍肯定公眾參與的重要性。雖然大眾的意見可能偏頗，而且不太能夠啟發建築設計，建築師仍認同大眾的意見具價值。這個虛偽的姿態可被理解成源自一種罪惡感：創作一張油畫只需要空白的畫布及顏料，但建築創作卻需要大量資源，而當中大部分都並非建築師所有。與存放於藝術家工作室的油畫不同，建築對其所在的環境亦有極大的影響。相對鼓勵公眾參與建築設計，在建築設計中強調個人創意因此在道德上較薄弱，而且政治不正確。即使建築師似乎也並不認為自己擁有權利為一

convinced that they are entitled to the right to exploit public resources merely for the sake of their own creativity. Perhaps this sense of guilt, concomitant with the creative desire to produce architecture, has pushed the profession to advocate public participation as a means of confession.

Public participation in architecture has been largely understood as a process in which the general public expresses opinions about an architectural design before it materializes in its physical context. Articulating informed opinions that could influence the design usually requires a certain level of architectural knowledge, and architecture writings have an essential role in equipping the general public with the language required to participate in architectural discourse. People can often relate more easily to written explanations, so architecture writings, transmitted through journalism to the public, supplement architectural drawings and help translate ideas from the architectural discipline to the general public. The narratives provided by architecture writings offer a window for people to understand arguments in an otherwise impenetrable architectural discourse. By providing the language for communicating these arguments, architecture writings become an agency for creating architecture, accessible to the public at large. At the same time, they document the discourse on architecture, providing an alternative mapping of architecture's historical development. The architectural writings analyzed in this book, selected from different periods, can thus be seen as a historical archive of China's architectural development.

While architecture writings open up the potential for public participation that could truly influence architectural design, participation still remains closed to those unable to comprehend the architectural discourse. The analysis in this book supports the conclusion that this has been, and remains, the situation in China. It is also reasonable to believe that China is not alone in facing this "lack" of public participation in architecture. However, if we expand our view of architecture beyond the construction of physical edifices, the definition of public participation can be similarly expanded. Recalling St. Paul's Cathedral as the backdrop of the Occupy London protest movement, I would suggest that public participation in architecture could simply mean the way a space is used by the general public. Inhabiting a space already defines and transforms it, placing it in a unique context where people act and interact. Going back to square one, perhaps the ultimate form of public participation in architecture is simply the interpretation of a space through its use. While few of us have the opportunity to influence the physical form of architecture, we all have the freedom to respond to a space and define it ourselves. Architecture writings also record these subtle architectural encounters, which were never planned on the drawing board. They record our voices in architecture. They record the built, and more importantly, the unbuilt.

Sylvia Chan Man-ha
Hong Kong, June 2012

己創意剝奪大眾資源。或許是這種隨建築創作而來的罪惡感，令建築專業以鼓吹公眾參與作為一種告解。

　　建築的公眾參與一般被視為大眾在建築建成以前，就設計發表意見的過程。要組成可以影響設計的中肯意見，通常需要一定程度的建築知識。建築寫作擔當重要角色，令大眾得到參與建築論述的語言。由於大眾比較容易理解文字，透過傳媒接觸大眾的建築寫作成了建築製圖的補充說明，協助向公眾詮釋建築界別的想法。建築寫作中的陳述提供一個媒介，讓一般大眾明白本來不可被理解的建築論述的論點。透過提供溝通論點的語言，建築寫作成為一項公眾也可使用的建築創作工具。同時，建築寫作紀錄了建築論述，為建築的歷史發展提供另一個圖譜。本書分析的文章選自不同時期，因此可被視為中國建築發展的歷史檔案庫。

　　儘管建築寫作開闢了可能性，令公眾參與並真正影響建築設計，但是未能明白建築論述的人士仍然未能參與建築設計。如本書所述，這正是中國一直至今的情況，而似乎中國並非單獨「欠缺」公眾參與建築設計的例子。不過，如果我們視建築為超越興建建築物實體的專業，我們可以更廣泛定義建築的公眾參與。想到聖保羅大教堂成了「佔領倫敦」示威活動的背景，我認為建築的公眾參與可以僅被詮釋成一般大眾對空間的運用。佔領一個空間其實已經定義並改變了空間，將空間置於一個有人物進行活動的環境。話說回來，或許公眾參與建築的極致，就是僅僅透過使用空間以詮釋空間。儘管我們之中只有少數人有機會影響建築的實體形態，我們卻都有自由去回應及定義空間。建築寫作紀錄了這些從未於圖板上計劃的微妙建築互動。寫作紀錄了我們就建築設計想表達的一切。寫作紀錄了那些建成的建築物，更重要的，它們紀錄了未建成的。

陳曼霞

香港，2012年6月

前言

速寫建築：

一九四九年以來的中國建築寫作與創建

AN ARCHITECTURE'S DISCOURSE: CHINA

To talk about "harmony" and "civilization" and to promote a "scientific concept of development" inside of a blatant sex toy is the height of irony! And for such a device to be standing in the capital of an ancient civilization brings shame onto our ancestors!

– comment of a netizen on the CCTV Headquarters, 23 February 2009[1]

In August 2009, a commentary which criticized the architectural design of the China Central Television Headquarters for looking like genitals appeared on the internet, and the building's architect, Rem Koolhaas, was accused of making fun of the Chinese. This commentary sparked a debate among architects, academics and the general public in newspapers, magazines, and websites across China. Koolhaas denied the erotic associations of the building, and his response was reported in the mass media.

Such a debate would have been inconceivable in China during the Maoist era, when all realms of society were manipulated by the government to strengthen Mao's rule. Writings concerning the CCTV headquarters are prominent examples that illuminate how the discourse on architecture in China is now taking shape. By looking at a series of seminal architecture writings since 1949, this book examines the discourse on architecture in China from 1949 to the present, as the country has transformed itself from a closed Communist regime into a state capitalist country. After the

founding of the People's Republic of China in 1949, Mao Zedong led the country under the banner of socialist ideology. In 1978, Deng Xiaoping assumed leadership of China, introducing fundamental changes to the economic system that included a greater reliance on market forces, though without shedding the "socialist" label. The new approach to economic management was modeled on state capitalism, featuring "less direct government involvement in enterprises, a major overhaul of the legal system with emphasis on commercial law to adjudicate contract disputes, moves to establish a more realistic pricing system, further reforms of the wage and bonus systems to provide incentives to boost production."[2] Concomitant with the economic transformation were changes in the discourse on architecture in China. Thomas A. Markus, an architecture theoretician with a special interest in language and texts about buildings who teaches Building Science at the University of Strathclyde Glasgow, has argued persuasively in his book *Words Between the Spaces: Buildings and Language* that changes in the writings on architecture over time are often related to broader social

1   http://www.wyzxsx.com/Article/Class12/200902/69531.html. The quote was translated by danwei.org.

2   Davies 1979, p.44

建築論述：中國

在一個赤裸裸的性交道具裡講「和諧」，話「文明」，促「科學發展觀」，具有莫大的諷刺意義！在一個文明古國的首都公然擺上這樣的道具，丟祖宗的臉！強烈呼籲追究相關決策者的法律責任！

— 一名網民對中央電視台新總部大樓的評價，2009年2月23日[1]

2009年8月，中國內地互聯網絡流傳一則評論，批評中央電視台新總部大樓及毗連的電視文化中心造型猶如人體生殖器，其建築師雷姆·庫哈斯 (Rem Koolhaas) 更被指企圖透過設計挪揄中國人。這則評論引發建築師、建築界學者以至普羅大眾在內地的報章、雜誌以及互聯網上，進行一連串激烈辯論。庫哈斯否認央視總部大樓的設計有色情含義，而他對有關評論的回應，受到了媒體廣泛報道。

上述討論在毛澤東時期的中國，根本不可想像，因為當時中國社會的各層面均受政府操控，以鞏固毛澤東的權力。就央視新總部大樓的討論，正好反映建築論述 (discourse on architecture) 如何在中國逐漸形成。本書將透過研究一系列具代表性的建築寫作文本，探討自1949年至今，亦即中國由封閉的共產政權轉變成國家資本主義社會期間，中國的建築論述如何不斷演化。1949年，中華人民共和國成立，毛澤東以社會主義思想統治國家。1978年，在鄧小平領導下，中國雖然仍然稱作社會主義國家，但其經濟體系出現了徹底改革，變成市場主導。新的經濟體系以國家資本主義為藍本，標榜「政府較少對企業作直接干預；法律制度重大改革，強調以商業法調解合約糾紛；建設合理訂價系統的措施；改革薪金及花紅發放機制，提高生產動力。」[2]期間，中國的建築論述亦出現了相應變化。如專注研究建築語言及文本、於英國格拉斯哥史崔克萊大學任教建造科學的建築理論學家托瑪斯·馬庫斯 (Thomas A. Markus) 於《字裡行間：建築及語言》(Words Between the Spaces: Buildings and Language) 一書所述，建築寫作文本的改變通常與更廣泛的社會改變有關。[3]《速寫建築》透過討論中國建築寫作文本的轉變，以反映中國建築的設計與建造的相應變化，以及有關變化對城市面貌的影響。本書並非旨在為中國的建築風格編寫一個系譜，但會主力探討中國的建築論述，以及論述與在中國實踐建築之間的互動關係。本書所指的建築寫作文本包括建築專業人士及一

1　http://www.wyzxsx.com/Article/Class12/200902/69531.html.

2　Davies 1979, p.44
3　Markus 2002, p.41

changes.[3] *Writing In(to) Architecture*, by discussing the changes in writings on architecture, registers corresponding changes in China's architectural design and construction, as well as how such changes have influenced the cityscapes of the country. This book does not aim to give a genealogy of the styles of architecture in China, but focuses on the discourse on architecture and its interaction with the way architecture is practiced. In this book, the term "architecture writings" is used to refer to writings in architectural journalism available to architectural professionals and the general public. British architect Hugh Casson, whose writing and broadcasting about 20th century design were highly influential, identified four main functions of architectural journalism: first, to give a full and accurate record of important or interesting new buildings; second, to provide technical information for the use of all those working in the building industry; third, to provide adequate space for criticism; fourth, to guide opinions and initiate ideas.[4] In other words, one main function of architectural journalism is to provide a place for discourse on architecture. Past architecture writings thus constitute an archive recording how the discourse on architecture has changed.

3   Markus 2002, p.41
4   Casson 1968, p.259-260

"Illusions about CCTV's 'Pornographic Gate'," *Y Weekend*, Vol.179, 27 August 2009
《央视大楼的『色情門』假象》，《青年周末》179期，2009年8月27日

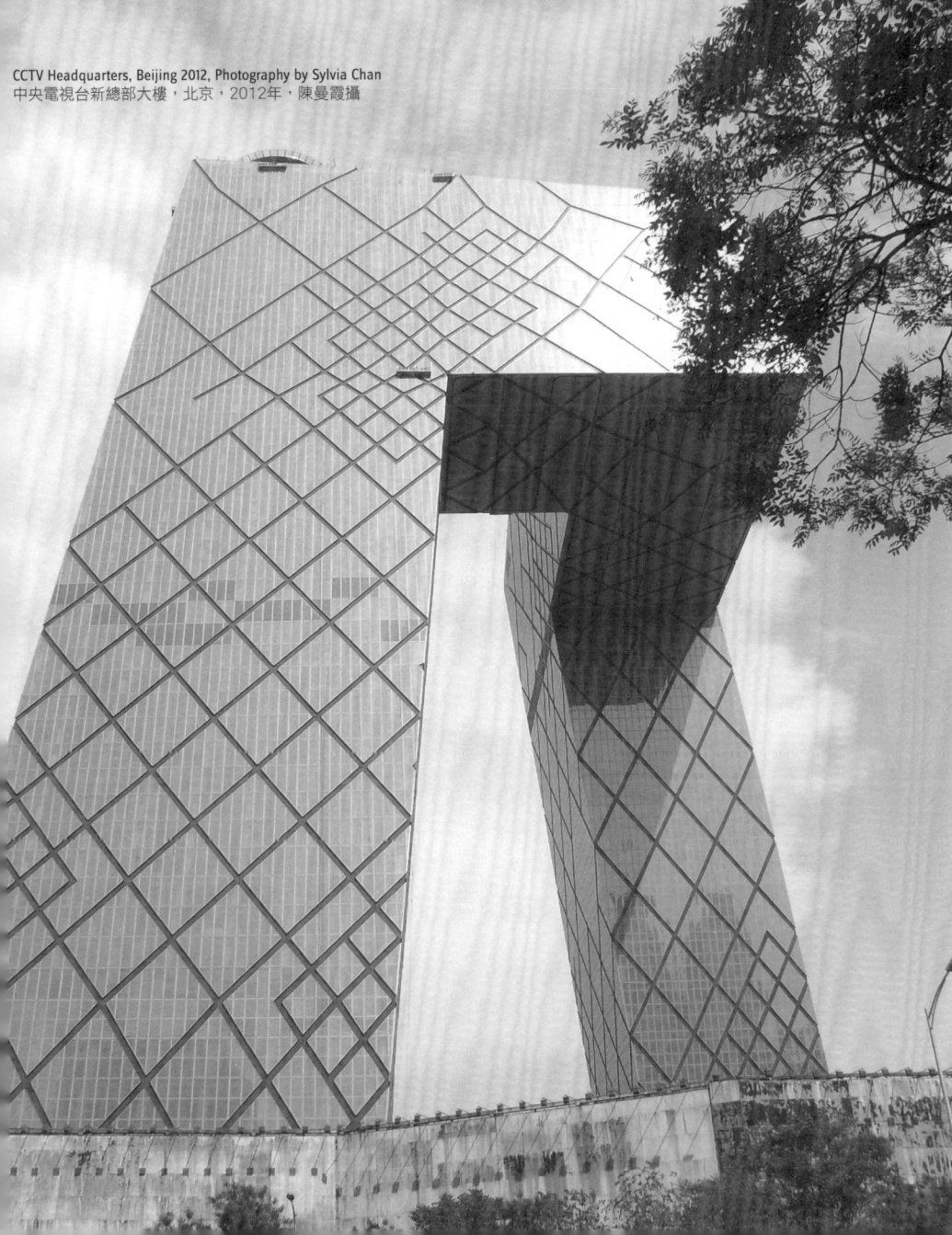

CCTV Headquarters, Beijing 2012, Photography by Sylvia Chan
中央電視台新總部大樓，北京，2012年，陳曼霞攝

般大眾可接觸到的建築相關文章。如英國建築師兼著名作家及廣播員休・卡森 (Hugh Casson) 所述，建築相關文章有四項主要功能：第一、詳盡並精確地紀錄重要或有趣的新建築物；第二、為建築界從業員提供有用的技術資訊；第三、提供一個評論空間；第四、引領意見及發動思潮。[4]換言之，建築相關文章的其中一項主要功能，是提供一個建築論述的場域。建築相關文章因此可被視作一個「檔案室」，紀錄建築論述的轉變。

目前，建築學術界已出現關於中國建築創建自1949年的發展的文獻。彼德・羅(Peter G. Rowe) 與關晟合著的《承傳與交融 ─ 探中國近現代建築的本質與形式》 (Architecture Encounters with Essence and Form in Modern China)、朱劍飛的 《中國當代建築：歷史的批判》 (Architecture of Modern China: a Historical Critique)、以及薛求理的 《建造革命：1980年以來的中國建築》 (Building a Revolution: Chinese Architecture since 1980) 均詳細研究了中國自1949年或以前，直至千禧年以後的建築創建。這些文獻紀錄了在中國社會政治氣候的變化下中國建築創建的變遷，顯示這些變遷如何影響中國建築師的地位，以及建築物的具體設計與建造。

不過，有關中國建築寫作文本演變的文獻則較為欠奉，特別是關於建築寫作文本如何影響建築實踐的文獻。有關文獻甚少在中國廣泛發表，當中主要包括中國大學研究生論文，而這些論文通常僅籠統地介紹中國的各種建築專業期刊[5]及當中的資訊，提供內容概要，並以統計學的手法分析專業期刊的資訊量。[6]建築學術界存有較多關於建築評論的研究，普遍以書籍及

4　Casson 1968, p.259-260
5　專業期刊意指刊載某專業的總體研究或意見的刊物，普遍由全國性的學術或專業聯會出版。(Crysler 2003, p.14)
6　請參考饒佳林著的《我國當前大眾傳播下專業建築批評的現狀研究》、蔣妙菲著的《建築雜誌在中國》及李凌燕著的《從當代中國建築期刊看當代中國建築的發展》。

Currently, there is literature that traces the development of architectural design and construction in China since 1949. *Architecture Encounters with Essence and Form in Modern China* by Peter G. Rowe and Seng Kuan, *Architecture of Modern China: a Historical Critique* by Zhu Jianfei, and *Building a Revolution: Chinese Architecture since 1980* by Charlie Q.L. Xue are comprehensive studies of China's architecture design and construction from 1949 (or earlier) until after the millennium. This literature records the changes in architecture design and construction in relation to the socio-political changes in China, registering how those changes affected both the status of architects and the ways in which architectural artefacts were designed and produced.

However, there is relatively little research about the evolution of architecture writings in China during this period, especially about the influence of those writings on the actual practice of architecture. Literature about architecture writings does not seem to be published or accessible in China, aside from the theses of university graduate students. These graduate theses usually provide general studies of the types of field journals[5] available in China, giving a brief summary of the content of different field journals and using statistical approaches to analyze the amount of information available in the journals.[6] There are also studies of architectural criticism available in books and theses which give an overview of the characteristics of architectural criticism in China.[7] However, this literature only gives a generic account of the development of architecture writings in China without analyzing specific articles. How the texts of architecture writings change in relation to the transformation of architectural design and construction does not seem to have been explored.

This book does not aim to provide a comprehensive overview of architecture writings from 1949 until the present. Instead it studies specific examples in both field journals and the mass media that mark some unique characteristics of the discourse on architecture in different periods of history. As Markus puts it, "the experience and understanding of buildings are always and inevitably mediated by language and discourse and the judgments in circulation about a particular phenomenon may

---

5   Field journals are publications that represent the totality of research and opinion in a particular field; they are typically published by national academic or professional associations. (Crysler 2003, p.14)
6   See "Architectural Criticism on the Mass Communication Environment" by Rao Jialin, "Architectural Magazines in China" by Jiang Miaofei, and "The Observation of the Development of Contemporary Chinese Architecture Through Contemporary Chinese Architectural Journals" by Li Lingyan.
7   See *Chuang zuo yu xing shi: dang dai Zhongguo jian zhu ping lun* by Zeng Zhaofen, *Jian zhu bai jia ping lun ji* edited by Yang Yongsheng, "Research on the Practice and Communication of Contemporary Architecture Criticism in China" by Cheng Xiaoxi, and "The Research on Contemporary Chinese Architectural Criticism" by Liu Dongmei.

大學研究生論文的形式發表，概論中國建築評論的特徵。[7]不過，上述的文獻均僅僅提供了中國建築寫作文本或評論的發展概要，並無分析個別建築寫作文本的具體文字及寫作手法，因此未能精確反映建築寫作文本如何隨著建築創建的改變而更迭。

本書並非旨在提供建築寫作文本自1949年至今的詳細發展概要，卻專注研究專業期刊及大眾媒體當中，反映不同歷史時期建築論述個別特徵的建築寫作文本。如馬庫斯所述：「人們對於建築物的感受與理解，往往不可避免地受語言及論述左右，而對於一種現象的普遍評價，也可能塑造出人們在現實中對這種現象的反應。」[8]透過剖析寫作文本，本書提供一個新視點，探討中國建築創建自1949年的演變。《速寫建築》旨在透過研究建築論述，從另一角度審視中國建築創建的情況，同時也探討建築專業人士以至一般大眾有關建築的討論。本書以線性敘事手法鋪排，討論中國建築論述隨著時間的演變。自1949年以來，中國建築論述出現數之不盡的微妙變化，而1978年 — 中國改革開放的一年，可被視為中國建築論述的轉捩點。

7　請參考曾昭奮著的《創作與形式: 當代中國建築評論》、楊永生編的《建築百家評論集》、程曉喜著的《中國當代建築評論的發展及傳播研究》及劉冬梅著的《中國建築評論的現狀研究》。

8　Markus 2002, p.93

also shape responses to it in material reality."[8] By dissecting the texts, this book introduces a new lens through which one can examine architecture in China since 1949. *Writing In(to) Architecture* provides an alternative mapping of the development of architecture in China by studying the discourse on architecture, registering not only how architectural works have been designed and constructed, but also how they have been discussed. The texts studied in this book are all in Chinese and have been translated by myself. Some field journals published in the 1990s and after have English titles and abstracts, and such English titles are used. This book adopts a linear narrative structure in discussing changes in the discourse on architecture in China over time. It pinpoints the year 1978, when China's reform and opening began, as a significant moment of change, though with an awareness that more subtle changes occurred throughout the span of time studied.

8   Markus 2002, p.93

Mausoleum of Mao Zedong, Beijing, 1976, Photography by Sylvia Chan
毛主席紀念堂，北京，1976年，陳曼霞攝

ARCHITECTURAL JOURNALISM IN CHINA: AN OVERVIEW

Architectural journalism has a longer history in the west than in China. As early as 1907, the importance of architectural journalism had been pointed out in the *Journal of the Royal Institute of British Architects*, which stated that "the modern architect has been evolved concurrently with the growth of professional journalism; the two have developed side by side."[9] However, journalistic architecture writings did not appear in China until the 1930s. This book studies specific examples of architecture writings published after 1949, while giving a brief account of the architectural journalism of China in the pre-1949 period.

Field journals on architecture have been published in China since the 1930s. *Bulletin of the Society for Research in Chinese Architecture*, published by the Society for Research in Chinese Architecture, was the first field journal on architecture in China. It was a quarterly journal published between 1930 and 1945, and mainly contained articles about research on traditional Chinese architecture. *The Chinese Architect* and *The Builder*, which aimed to introduce western construction technologies to China, were published by the Society of Chinese Architects and the Shanghai Architectural Association, respectively, beginning in 1931 and 1932. Both journals ceased publication in 1937 due to the Second Sino-Japanese War. In 1936, China New Architecture Group, which promoted modern architecture in China, published *Die Architektur*, which included articles about functionalism and modern architecture. *Die Architektur*'s publication was interrupted between 1939 and 1941 due to the Second Sino-Japanese War, and the journal ceased publication in August 1949, two months before the People's Republic of China (PRC) was established in October of the same year.[10]

From the establishment of the PRC until China reopened its doors in 1978 at the end of the Cultural Revolution,[11] architecture design and construction in China was completely manipulated by the government. During that period, there were only two field journals on architecture in China — *Architectural Journal*, published by the Architectural Society of China starting in 1954; and *Construction and Architecture*, published by the Construction Engineering Department beginning the same year. In the preface of the first issue of *Architectural Journal*, the journal defined itself as "an academic journal that publishes directive essays on theories of architecture and important essays on construction technology." Its aim was "to promote the directions of the government," introduce the architecture of Russia to the PRC and provide

---

9   Adams 1907, p.313

10   Jiang 2004, p.20-26

11   The official launch of "four modernizations" was announced in December 1978 at the Third Plenum of the 11th Central Committee. The "four modernizations" included areas of agriculture, industry, national defense, and science and technology, and essentially stressed economic self-reliance of industries in the four areas. Since 1978, the PRC has adopted open door policies and allowed international trade and foreign direct investment.

中國建築傳媒：概要

相較中國，西方的建築傳媒有更悠久的歷史。早於1907年，《英國皇家建築師協會期刊》(Journal of the Royal Institute of British Architects) 已指出建築傳媒的重要性：「當代建築師與專業建築傳媒同步成長；兩者共同發展。」，不過中國的建築相關文章自1930年代才開始出現。本書將研究1949年以後出版的個別建築寫作文本，並簡介1949年以前的中國建築傳媒概況。

中國的建築專業期刊自1930年代開始出版，中國營造學社出版的《中國營造學社匯刊》是中國首部建築專業期刊。自1930年至1945年，《中國營造學社匯刊》以季刊形式出版，主要刊登有關中國傳統建築的研究。《中國建築》及《建築月刊》分別於1931年及1932年由中國建築師學會及上海市建築協會出版，旨在向中國介紹西方的建造技術；兩部期刊均受抗日戰爭影響，於1937年停刊。1936年，中國新建築社出版《新建築》，發表有關實用主義及當代建築的文章。《新建築》的出版同樣受抗日戰爭影響，於1939年至1941年間中斷，並終於1949年8月，即中華人民共和國成立前兩個月停刊。[10]

在中華人民共和國成立以後、1978年文化大革命完結及中國改革開放[11]以前的一段期間，中國建築創建完全由政府操控。當時只有兩部建築專業期刊 ── 中國建築學會於1954年出版的《建築學報》，以及同年由原建築工程部出版的《建築》。根據《建築學報》的發刊辭，《建築學報》「內容主要是指導性的理論論文和重要的技術論文」，而學報有明確目的，「它是為國家總路線服務的」，向中國介紹蘇聯的建築，並提供一個評論中共建築創建發展的平台。學報的主要對象是建築師，同時亦希望引發大眾與建築師討論建築。[12]《建築學報》於1965年、以及1966年11月至1973年9月期間，受文化人革命影響而停刊。直至1981年變成月刊以前，《建築學報》每年不定期發行。另外《建築》主要刊登有關建設業行業管理及建築企業經營的文章，這類文章與本書討論的建築創建並無直接關係，因此本書不會討論《建築》一刊。

9　Adams 1907, p.313

10　蔣妙菲 2004, p.20-26
11　1978年12月，十一屆三中全會正式宣佈重新啟動1950年代末始提出的「四個現代化」。「四個現代化」包括工業現代化、農業現代化、國防現代化及科學技術現代化，強調這四個範疇的產業實行自負盈虧。自1978年，中華人民共和國採納對外開放政策，放寬對外貿易及外商直接投資的限制。
12　《建築學報》，1954(01), p.3

a forum for criticism on the development of the PRC's architectural production. The target audience was architects, and the journal aimed to launch discussions on architecture that included architects and the general public.[12] *Architectural Journal*'s publication was interrupted in 1965, and between November 1966 and September 1973, due to the Cultural Revolution. The number of issues published each year fluctuated until it became a monthly journal in 1981. The focus of *Construction and Architecture* has been on the management of the architectural industry rather than architecture design and construction; thus it is not discussed in this book.

Architecture writings in the mass media during the pre-1978 era mainly included articles in newspapers published by media institutions that were part of governmental organizations. These institutions were highly centralized and strictly supervised, and were used by the government to publicize the ideology of the Chinese Communist Party (CCP).[13]

With Deng Xiaoping assuming national leadership in 1978 after the end of the Cultural Revolution, the "four modernizations" program and the open-door policies were introduced.

By the early 1980s, the state could no longer afford to fully subsidize media operations that had been monopolized by the CCP since 1949, and the market mechanism was introduced into the media. Under the challenge of market forces, "state control retreated, step by step, from areas with the fewest political implications — entertainment, popular culture, information about daily life, social news and intellectual debates."[14] Architectural journalism, an area with relatively few political implications, began to develop rapidly in the 1980s and an increasing number of field journals on architecture were established during the early 1980s. Among the field journals available since that era, *Architectural Journal, Huazhong Architecture, New Architecture, Time + Architecture* and *World Architecture* have been listed as core journals by *Source Journals for Chinese Scientific and Technical Papers and Citations, Chinese Core Journal List*, and *China Journals Full-text Database* (the three major citation indices that allow a researcher to identify which journals have been cited most frequently and are most influential). Apart from *Architectural Journal*, the other four all began publication in the 1980s

---

12   *Architectural Journal*, 1954(01), p.3
13   Liu 2003, p.23

14   Liu 2003, p.8-9

1978年以前，在大眾傳媒出現的建築寫作文本主要包括刊載於報章的建築相關文章，而這些報章均由隸屬政府的傳媒機構出版。這些傳媒機構由中央政府嚴密操控，是中國共產黨用作宣傳其理念及思想的主要工具。[13]

1978年，文化大革命結束，鄧小平掌管全國統治，實行「四個現代化」及改革開放政策。自1949年以來，中國共產黨一直壟斷傳媒機構的營運，但自1980年代初期起，政府無法繼續全數資助傳媒機構，傳媒架構於是引入開放的市場機制。在市場力量的挑戰下，「政府的操控逐少縮小，並先從政治含意較少的範疇消失 ── 娛樂、流行文化、生活資訊、社會新聞及學術辯論。」[14]建築傳媒是政治含意較少的範疇之一，故於1980年代開始迅速發展，新發行的專業期刊紛紛在1980年代初開始出版。在1980年代出版的專業期刊當中，《建築學報》、《華中建築》、《新建築》、《時代建築》及《世界建築》均被中國科技論文統計源期刊、中文核心期刊要目總覽及中國期刊全文數據庫列為核心期刊（三項指引提供快速評價期刊的重要性及影響力的標準）。除《建築學報》外，其餘四部專業期刊均於1980年代創刊 ──《世界建築》於1980年創刊、《華中建築》及《新建築》於1983年創刊、《時代建築》於1984年創刊。《世界建築》由清華大學創辦，旨在向中國介紹國外的建築理論及建築創建發展。《華中建築》由中南建築設計院創辦，推廣將中國特色融入當代建築。《新建築》由華中科技大學出版，主要介紹中國新一代建築師的作品。《時代建築》由同濟大學出版，主要刊登中國建築師的作品及理論研究。

1990年代初，西方的建築專業期刊甚少在中國出現。當時，在中國出現的西方建築雜誌，通常是沒有圖片的盜版影印本。較完整的彙集通常只在大學圖書館出現。1992年，清華大學的教授將 Domus 的選段翻譯成中文出版，但僅出版了數期，並只在北京發行。[15]外國出版商的專業期刊主要於2000年後才於中國流通。《建築細部》(Detail) 中文版由2003年開始出版，提供德國版雜誌部分文章的中文翻譯，以及中國建築作品的個案分析。a+u 中文版及《建築素

13　Liu 2003, p.23
14　Liu 2003, p.8-9
15　Greco 2008, p.93

— *World Architecture* in 1980, *Huazhong Architecture* and *New Architecture* in 1983, and *Time + Architecture* in 1984. *World Architecture*, published by Tsinghua University, aims at introducing to China both the architectural theories and the design and construction developments in foreign countries. *Huazhong Architecture* is published by Central-South Architectural Design Institute, and promotes the incorporation of Chinese characteristics into modern architecture. *New Architecture*, published by Huazhong University of Science and Technology, focuses on works by young Chinese architects. *Time + Architecture* is published by Tongji University and mostly contains articles introducing design works and theoretical studies by Chinese architects.

In the early 1990s, western architectural magazines were rarely found in China. Those that were available were often duplicated by cyclostyle, without photographs. More complete collections were available in the libraries of universities. In 1992, professors at Tsinghua University translated excerpts from the Italian architecture magazine *Domus*, but only a few issues were published and they were distributed exclusively in Beijing.[15] Architectural magazines from foreign publishers became available in China after 2000. *Detail*, which provides translations of articles from the original German version as well as case studies on architecture in China, began in 2003. Chinese editions of *a+u* and *El Croquis* began in 2005, with articles translated from the Japanese and Spanish editions. In 2006, *Domus China*, published entirely in Chinese, was established; two-thirds of the magazine is a Chinese translation of the Italian version, but it also has original Chinese articles about China's architectural scene.

The open-door policies of 1978 led to a media boom in China, and more writings on architecture are now available in newspapers and general interest magazines, some of which have regular columns on architecture. Features on architecture can also be found in major lifestyle magazines, including *Architecture and Design* and *The Outlook Magazine*. Since the late 1990s, the internet has become another popular platform for architecture writings.

The examples of pre-1978 architecture writings in this book have been chosen from *Architectural Journal* and from newspapers, in particular *People's Daily*, the most widely read newspaper at that time. Examples from the post-1978 era have been selected after extensive reading of articles from the five core journals mentioned above, as well as *Domus China*,

15   Greco 2008, p.93

描》 (El Croquis) 均於2005年出版，刊登日本版及西班牙版期刊的文章中譯本。2006年，完全以中文出版的 Domus China 創立，雜誌的三分之二是意大利版的中譯本，而雜誌亦特別刊載有關中國建築界的文章。

1978年的改革開放政策引發中國媒體迅速發展，更多建築寫作文本於報章及一般消閒雜誌出現，當中部分刊物更開設建築專欄。部分生活雜誌，如《設計新潮》及《新視線》等，亦有刊登有關建築的專題。1990年代末起，互聯網亦成為刊登建築寫作文本的另一個重要平台。

在本書分析的建築寫作文本中，1978年以前的建築寫作文本均選取自《建築學報》及報章，特別是當時最受廣泛閱讀的《人民日報》。1978年以後的建築寫作文本則選取自《建築學報》、《華中建築》、《新建築》、《時代建築》及《世界建築》五部核心期刊、Domus China、內地暢銷報章、雜誌以及互聯網。[16]本書分析的建築寫作文本均反映當時建築論述的

特性，以求捕捉其所屬時代的精粹。建築寫作文本並無絕對明確的分類，但為便於分析，本書將中國的建築寫作文本分成三大類別：政府宣傳性文章 ── 即明確以為政府宣傳為目的的文章、介紹性文章 ── 即介紹重要或有趣的新建築、或提供有關建築界的資訊、或向業界提供技術資訊的文章，以及評論 ── 即表達對建築的判斷、獨特的見解或有關的回應的文章，[17]其內容可能關於建築創建方針、某座建築物或建築理論。本書將分析這三類建築寫作文本自1949年以來的轉變。

16　本書並未選取 El Croquis 及 a+u 中文版的文章，因為此兩部期刊僅刊登西班牙版及日本版的中譯本。本書分析的1990年代以後出版的報章文章，均選取自《北京晚報》、《楚天都市報》、《廣州日報》、《人民日報》、《齊魯晚報》、《南方都市報》、《新民晚報》、《羊城晚報》及《揚子晚報》。這些報章是中國2006年十大暢銷報章。本書分析的雜誌包括《設計新潮》、《新視線》、《Vision青年視覺》及《青年周末》，而網站則包括 abbs.com 及 far2000.com

17　Rendell 2007, p.152

large-circulation Chinese newspapers, magazines and websites.[16] Articles were selected based on their relevance to the characteristics of discourse in a particular era, in an effort to capture the essence of the time period. While aware that there is often no clear-cut distinction between different forms of writings, this book categorizes architecture writings in China into three main forms: government propaganda writings — articles that explicitly serve the purpose of government propaganda; introductory articles — articles that give information about important or interesting new buildings or architectural practices, or provide technical information for the use of those working in the building industry; and commentaries — opinion articles that give judgments, discriminating points of view, or responses[17] about issues related to architecture, such as architectural principles, particular buildings, or architectural theories.

People's Daily, 17 November 1957
《人民日報》，1957年11月17日

16　Chinese editions of *El Croquis* and *a+u* are excluded in this book as they only have articles translated from the original editions of the magazines. Newspaper articles published since the 1990s have been selected from *Beijing Evening News, Chutian Metropolis Daily, Guangzhou Daily, People's Daily, Qilu Evening News, Southern Metropolis Daily, Xinmin Evening News, Yangcheng Evening News* and *Yangzi Evening News*. These newspapers were among the top ten most widely circulated newspapers in 2006. Magazines studied include *Architecture and Design, Vision, The Outlook Magazine* and *Y-Weekend*. Websites studied include abbs.com and far2000.com.

17　Rendell 2007, p.152

Architectural Journal, Issue 9, 1958
《建築學報》，9期，1958年

Time + Architecture, Issue 3, 2011
《時代建築》，3期，2011年

Xinmin Evening News, 16 January 2010
《新民晚報》，2010年1月16日

1949-1978

一九四九年至一九七八年

GOVERNMENT PROPAGANDA: WRITING TO MANIPULATE

In the Maoist era, articles in newspapers and *Architectural Journal* explicitly served the purpose of government propaganda, promoting principles for architecture that were set by the government. The target audience for these writings included both architectural professionals and the general public, and the government tried to manipulate their views to build support for the principles set by the state. The writings included reports on conferences of government officials and architects where the directions for architecture were discussed, as well as articles by both government officials and architects who promoted the government's views. Writings by architectural professionals who attempted to interpret the principles for architecture set by the government were also available in *Architectural Journal*.

Propaganda Writings in Newspapers

The Maoist government controlled the platforms where architecture writings appeared, and the content of articles in newspapers and *Architectural Journal* were either explicitly censored by the government, or were subject to the author's own careful self-censorship. Only writings that supported government opinions were published, and writings that questioned the government principles for architecture design and construction simply did not appear. The audience could only read views in line with those of the state; it was impossible for them to engage with the government in a debate about architectural principles.

"State Construction Committee Held the National Infrastructure Congress and Discussed the Preliminary Strategies and Basic Measures for Design, Architecture, and City Development," *People's Daily*, 8 March 1956
《國家建設委員會召開全國基本建設會議 — 討論了設計、建築、城市建設工作初步規劃和基本措施》，《人民日報》，1956年3月8日

政府宣傳：以文字操控

在毛澤東時期，報章及《建築學報》的部分文章均明確擔當為政府宣傳的功能，宣揚政府訂立的建築設計及建設方針。這些建築寫作文本以建築專業人士及大眾為對象，政府企圖透過建築寫作文本操控他們的意見，致使他們支持政府訂立的建築創建方針。這些建築寫作文本包括對政府官員及建築師的會議的報道，有關的會議討論內容均環繞建築創建方向；宣傳性的建築寫作文本亦包括政府官員及建築師撰寫推廣政府立場的文章。建築專業人士亦嘗試闡釋政府訂立的建築創建方針，並於《建築學報》發表相關文章。

報章上的宣傳性文章

在毛澤東時期，專制政權控制了所有建築寫作文本出現的平台，除了報章及《建築學報》的內容受政府審查外，建築寫作文本的作者小謹慎地自我審查，故只有支持政府立場的意見才得以出版；相反地，質疑或反對政府訂立的方針的文章都不會在報章或《建築學報》出現。讀者只能讀到與政府意見相符的論調，並不可能與政府辯論建築創建方針的合理性。

政府官員及建築師討論建築創建方針的會議報道、以至政府官員撰寫的文章，均清楚列明政府訂立的方針。這些文章採用一種直接的宣傳寫作手法：清楚列明建築創建方針，直接告訴讀者進行建築創建時，應採納甚麼態度或採取何種行動。這種宣傳寫作手法的用意，在於減少讀者可接觸到的不同選擇或可能性，簡化他們在決定採納何種意見之前所需經歷的思考過程，敦促讀者相信政府訂立的建築創建方針是唯一的選擇。1956年3月8日在《人民日報》出版、由新華社撰寫的《國家建設委員會召開全國基本建設會議 — 討論了設計、建築、城市建設工作初步規劃和基本措施》(《國家建設委員會》)，以及1956年10月10日在《人民日報》出版、由建築材料工業部部長賴際發撰寫的《大力增加建築材料新品種》均屬於此類文章。《國家建設委員會》一文明確指出應該「大力編制和推廣標準設計」，亦即將房屋、工廠等不同建築類型的設計範例應用於不同地方的不同項目，以節省設計的人力及降低成本，而標準設計在這些文章中，被描繪成唯一的設計方法。在文中，「必須」、「應該」及「要求」等字眼經常出現，以表示政府訂立的建築創建方針的權威性。例如文中提及編制標準設計時，指出「各設計部門和有關領導機關必須採取一切辦法來保證完成」，又指各設計部門「應該迅速清理已有的蘇聯標準設計，積極從蘇聯方面取得新的標準設計資料和圖紙」。文中亦指政府「要求」中國的設計人員向蘇聯專家學習。

有關建築創建方針的會議報道及政府官員撰寫的文章，往往會分析當時的建築創建狀況，

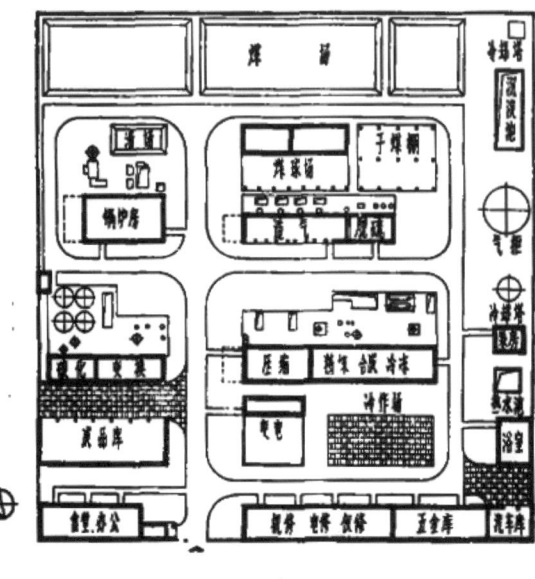

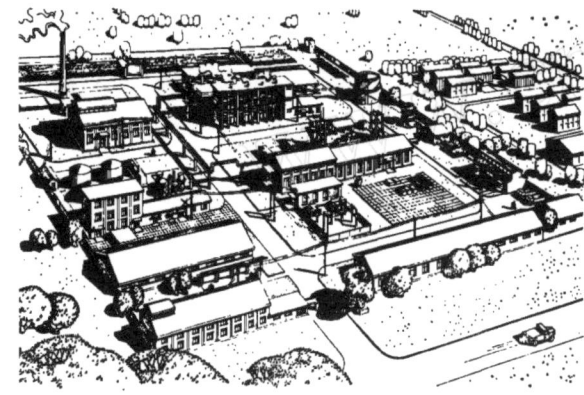

Reports on conferences and articles written by government officials stated clearly the government principles for architecture. The propaganda technique of telling the audience exactly what actions to take by directly stating the principles simplified the reader's decision-making process, eliminating any other possible choices. The audience was reminded that the directions set by the state were the only options available. Examples of such writings included "State Construction Committee Held the National Infrastructure Congress and Discussed the Preliminary Strategies and Basic Measures for Design, Architecture, and City Development" ("State Construction Committee") written by the government news agency Xinhua and published in *People's Daily* on 8 March 1956, and "Increase the New Types of Construction Materials Available" ("Increase") written by the head of the Ministry of Building Materials, Lai Jifa, and published in *People's Daily* on 10 October 1956. "State Construction Committee" clearly states that standard designs should be used, and standard designs are portrayed as the only design option available. Standard designs were designs for various building types, including housing and factories, which were used as prototypes to be applied to different projects in different places. Standard designs were promoted to save design manpower, thus lowering costs. "State Construction Committee" often uses terms such as "must," "should" and "require" to convey the authority of these architectural principles. For example, the article notes that all design departments

CLOCKWISE 順時針:

Plan, standard design for nitrogen phosphate fertilizer
factories, 1960s
合成氮廠通用設計平面圖，1960年代

Nitrogen phosphate fertilizer factory, Fujian, 1960s
氮肥廠，福建，1960年代

Nitrogen phosphate fertilizer factory, Guangxi, 1960s
氮肥廠，廣西，1960年代

Nitrogen phosphate fertilizer factory, Zhejiang, 1960s
氮肥廠，浙江，1960年代

Aerial plan, Standard design for nitrogen phosphate
fertilizer factories, 1960s
合成氮廠通用設計鳥瞰，1960年代

並對當時的狀況作出批評，從而點出政府訂立的方針可解決當時的問題。此論點通常由數據支持，表示政府訂立的方針乃基於對當時現狀的細心分析，並以「科學化」的數據為根基。例如《國家建設委員會》一文使用了大量數據支持國家應採用標準設計此論點，文中指：「煤炭工業部所屬各設計院，在今年所擔負的設計項目預計為4,500多項，經過交流圖紙的結果，有3,300項圖紙可以重複使用，這樣就可以節省出7,300多個設計工作日。」文中亦提及輕工業部和紡織工業部三年來由於採用標準設計，「節省了16萬個設計工作日」。不過，這些數據的來源並無根據，文中亦無資料說明節省出的設計工作日如何計算出來，這些數據因此未能向讀者引證標準設計的有效性，僅被用作標準設計的盲目宣傳。

除了政府通訊社或政府官員撰寫的文章外，只有同意政府論點的文章才可以在報章出版。這些主要由建築專業人士撰寫的文章因此是另一種宣傳政府思想的文章。政府利用這類文章，傳達建築專業人士支持政府訂立的建築創建方針這個訊息，並借專業人士的身份，令政府訂立的方針顯得更具權威及說服力。

在這類文章中，建築專業人士通常會重申政府的觀點，並承認自己的作品沒有遵照政府

"must use every single method" to ensure the use of standard designs, and "should proactively" gather drawings of the standard designs of Russia. It also states that the government "requires" the design practitioners of the PRC to learn from Russian experts.

In reports on conferences and articles written by government officials, the existing conditions in architecture were often analyzed and criticized, and it was commonly claimed that the principles set by the state were able to solve existing problems. Statistics were often used to support such claims, suggesting that the principles were based on careful analysis of existing conditions and were "scientifically" supported. For example, to promote the use of standard design, "State Construction Committee" states that among the 4,500 design projects of the Ministry of Coal Industry, more than 3,300 could use standard designs, and that the use of standard designs would save 7,300 working days. The article also asserts that the use of standard designs by two other ministries had saved 160,000 design working days in three years. However, no source is given for these statistics, and there is no information about how the savings in working days were calculated. The statistics serve less to inform the audience about the true efficiency of using standard designs, than to promote standard design regardless of its efficiency.

Aside from articles written by government news agencies and government officials, only articles

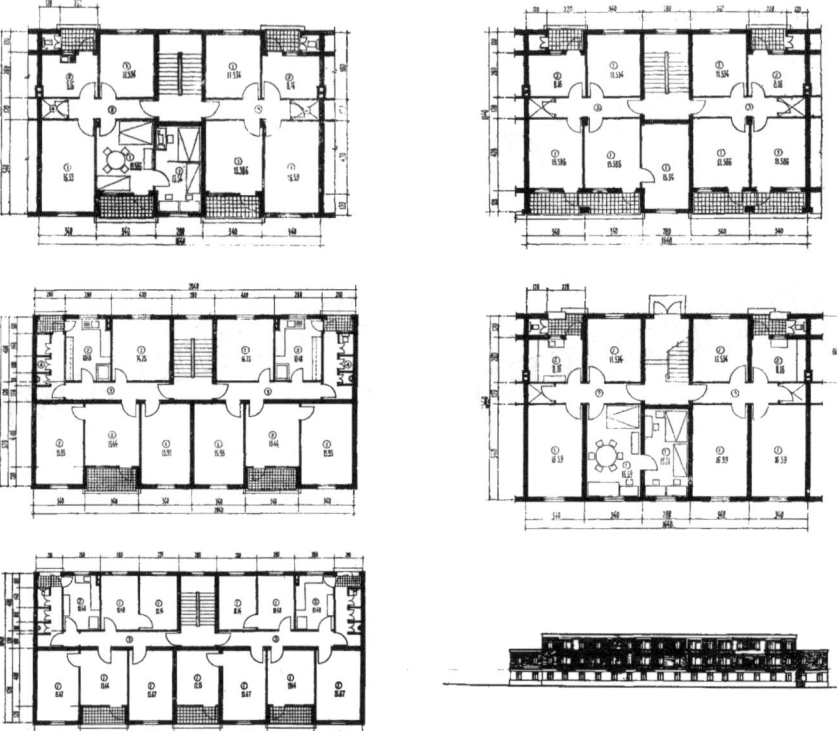

FROM TOP 最上起:
Plan, standard design for residential block, variation - five kaijian, Guangdong, 1950s
標準設計住宅平面圖，五開間單元，廣東，1950年代

Plan, standard design for residential block, variation - six kaijian, Guangdong, 1950s
標準設計住宅平面圖，六開間單元，廣東，1950年代

Plan, standard design for residential block, variation - seven kaijian, Guangdong, 1950s
標準設計住宅平面圖，七開間單元，廣東，1950年代

FROM TOP 最上起:
Plan, standard design for residential block, variation - west facing apartments, Guangdong, 1950s
標準設計住宅平面圖，西曬區設計，廣東，1950年代

Plan, standard design for residential block, variation - typhoon area, Guangdong, 1950s
標準設計住宅平面圖，颱風區設計，廣東，1950年代

Elevation, standard design for residential block, Guangdong, 1950s
標準設計住宅立面圖，廣東，1950年代

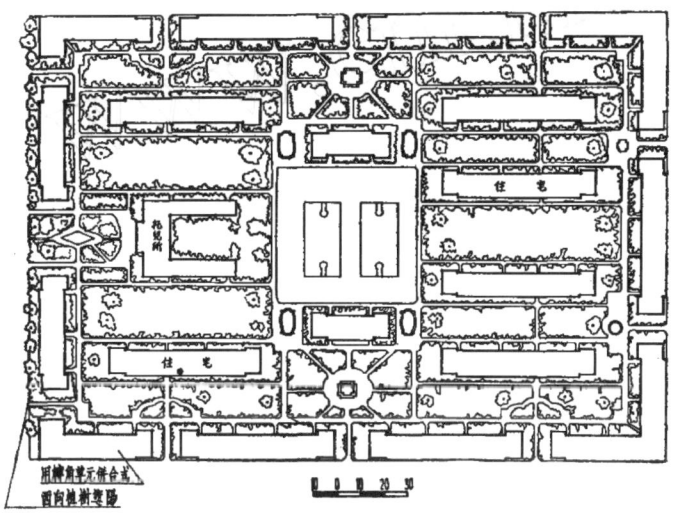

Overall plan, residential area with standard design blocks, Guangdong, 1950s
總體平面圖，標準設計住宅區，廣東，1950年代

訂立的方針，然後自責。遵照政府訂立的方針而實踐的建築方式，均被視為「正確」，一切其他方式都被視為「錯誤」，而建築專業人士往往在文章裡承認自己的「錯誤」。透過確定政府訂立的建築創建方針為「正確」，政府進一步令方針變得無可爭辯。不過，何謂「正確」或「錯誤」從未被確切定義。在由建築工程部北京工業建築設計院副院長汪季琦撰寫、於1955年5月8日在《人民日報》出版的《我在領導設計工作中的錯誤》一文中，汪季琦便引述1955年3月28日《人民日報》批評其領導的設計院的社論（《反對建築中的浪費現象》），並承認社論對設計院的指責「都是合乎事實的，都是十分正確的。」汪季琦指其領導的設計院「設計思想和設計工作的主要錯誤是嚴重地違反了『實用、經濟、在可能條件下注意美觀』的方針」，而「實用、經濟、在可能條件下注意美觀」是在1950年代惡劣經濟環境下，政府所提倡的建築創建方針之一。[18]汪季琦同意《人民日報》社論所指設計院的行徑「是對國家和人民的犯罪」，而他「有責任在這裡進行自我批評」及「大力進行標準設計，使正確設計思想的實現獲得技術上的保證。」

18　Xue 2006, p.4

that supported the views of the state could make their way into the newspapers. These articles, though often written by architectural professionals, were another form of government propaganda, promoting government architectural principles. Such articles were used to suggest that the government's principles were advocated by architectural professionals, making the principles appear more convincing and authoritative.

In such articles, architectural professionals often reiterated the government's architectural principles, condemning themselves and their own earlier works for not complying with them. Architectural practices that followed the principles were considered "right," while all others were considered "wrong." Architects admitted their "faults" in the articles. These assertions that government principles were "right" further promoted the indisputability of such principles, and there was no room for questioning what was "right" and what was "wrong." In "My Faults in My Design Leadership Work" ("My Faults") published in *People's Daily* on 8 May 1955, Wang Jiqi, head of the former China Architecture Design and Research Group, quotes a *People's Daily* editorial published on 28 March 1955 criticizing his design institute for making wasteful designs, and admits that the criticisms were "absolutely correct." Wang says the institute had betrayed the principle that buildings should be "functional, economical, and delightful if conditions permit," one of the main principles set under the

在《我在領導設計工作中的錯誤》中，汪季琦以「在1952年用了約每平方公尺200元翻修了(的)一座建築物」，以及「景山後面一個俱樂部的設計」，作為其領導的設計院「浪費」的例子。文中並未提及這兩座建築物的名稱，因此讀者無法知道汪季琦所指的是哪兩座建築物。換言之，建築專業人士撰寫的這類文章並不旨在向讀者提供資料，以便他們判斷建築師實踐的建築方式是否「錯誤」。這類文章旨在令讀者相信撰寫文章的建築專業人士的設計的確與政府訂立的方針相悖，造成了錯誤。換言之，這類文章只是一種工具，傳播政府訂立的建築創建方針為「正確」的信息。

《建築學報》的宣傳性文章

討論建築創建方針的會議報道、以及政府官員及建築專業人士撰寫的文章，除了在一般報章出版外，也在《建築學報》刊登。不過《建築學報》的文章主要由建築專業人士撰寫，並以較理論的層面討論政府訂立的方針，企圖定義這些方針所採用的字眼，令方針更為明確。毛

澤東時期政府推動的建築創建方針，主要包括「實用、經濟、在可能條件下注意美觀」及在中國建設「新社會主義風格」。[19]《建築學報》的建築寫作文本反映當時的建築專業人士分別嘗試闡釋這些方針所用字眼的含義，從而激起有關建築創建方針的實際意義的辯論。1955年《建築學報》出版、由同濟大學教授翟立林撰寫的《論建築藝術與美及民族形式》，[20]以及其後一連串的回應文章，反映了當時建築專業人士如何一方面宣揚政府訂立的方針，卻又同時按自己對方針的不同理解作出詮釋。[21]本書不會嘗試羅列不同作者在其文章發表的論點，反而希望透過這些文章，反映就建築創建方針所用字眼進行的辯論的特點。

儘管《建築學報》的政府宣傳性文章嘗試分析政府訂立的建築創建方針的含義，這些建築寫作文本仍以宣傳方針為目標。在《論建築藝術與美及民族形式》一文，翟立林在文中清楚表明，文章旨在「批判當時正在流行著的形式主義、復古主義的建築理論」。在50年代初，曾在國外於巴黎美術院派 (Beaux-Arts) 課程門下研習的建築師被徵召返回中華人民共和國服務。他們以巴黎美術院派的設計方式為中國創造出「民族形式，社會主義內容」，例如當時

19 Xue 2006, p.4
20 《建築學報》，1955(01), p.46-68
21 見著解 74.

harsh economic realities of the 1950s.[18] He describes the practices of his design institute as "sinful," and says he has "the responsibility to criticize himself" and "push forward the use of standard design." The article shows the absence of initiative among architectural professionals to argue with the government.

In "My Faults," Wang uses "a certain building that was renovated in 1952 at a cost of RMB200 per square meter" and "a clubhouse behind Jingshan" as examples of "wasteful works" designed by his institute. Most of his audience had no idea which two buildings Wang was referring to, because the names of the buildings are not given. Such writings were not meant to provide information that would enable the audience to make judgments about whether architects had in fact made mistakes. The articles left no room to question whether architectural professionals had been making mistakes by contradicting the design principles set by the government. The articles were merely tools to reinforce the idea that such principles were "right."

Model, Dormitory of Dianmen, Beijing, 1954, architecture exemplifying revivalism and national form
地安門機關宿舍大樓模型，北京，1954年，展示復古主義及民族形式的建築

18   Xue 2006, p.4

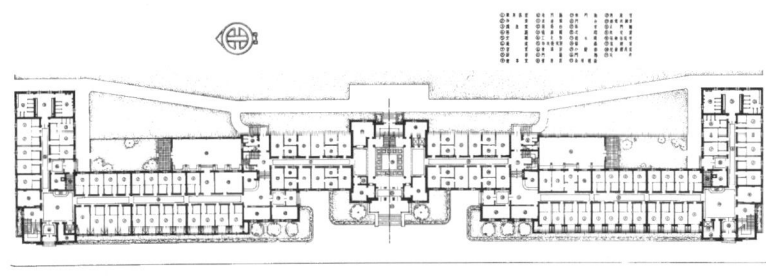

(above) Elevation, Dormitory of Dianmen, Beijing, 1954
（上）地安門機關宿舍大樓立面圖，北京，1954年

(below) Plan, Dormitory of Dianmen, Beijing, 1954
（下）地安門機關宿舍大樓平面圖，北京，1954年

具備中國傳統結構建築元素（特別是大屋頂）的建築物。[22]1955年，復古主義遭受政府抨擊，但由於當時並沒有對復古主義的確切定義，導致之後數年出現了關於「復古主義」及「民族形式」的意義的辯論。翟立林在文章開首，便強調該文乃根據「蘇聯全蘇建築工作會議及我國建築工程部召開的設計及施工工作會議的各種文件的精神加以修正補充」。[23]在通篇文章，翟立林於不同部分直接或間接地重申政府訂立的方針，例如他在文中表示：「我們的建築事業就不能不根據總路線任務的要求決定其方針政策」，[24]而他又直接指出「實用、經濟、在可能條件下注意美觀」是「根據過渡時期的具體條件所規定的正確的方針」。[25]另外翟立林亦指出「功能和技術的內容是首要的、是基本的，而思想意識的內容是次要的、是派生的。」[26]換言之，他以另一組字眼，重申「實用、經濟、在可能條件下注意美觀」這項方針。

在《建築學報》的宣傳性文章當中，以毛澤東為首的中共官員的意見，以及被中共官員

22　Zhu 2009, p.75
23　翟立林 1955, p.46
24　翟立林 1955, p.66
25　翟立林 1955, p.67
26　翟立林 1955, p.53

Propaganda Writings in *Architectural Journal*

Reports on conferences, as well as articles written by government officials and architects, also appeared in *Architectural Journal*. The journal distinguished itself, however, by regularly publishing writings by architectural professionals who discussed the principles for architecture set by the government at a more theoretical level, often trying to define the terms used in these principles. Two major principles promoted by the government in the Maoist era were that buildings should be "functional, economical, and delightful if conditions permit," and that architects should aim to create "a new socialist architectural style in China."[19] In *Architectural Journal*, architectural professionals tried to interpret the terms used in such principles, resulting in debates about their possible meanings. In 1955, *Architectural Journal* published an article titled "A Discussion on Architecture as Art in Relation to Aesthetics and National Form"[20] ("A Discussion") written by Zhai Lilin, professor of architecture at Tongji University. Zhai's article, together with the subsequent articles responding to "A Discussion," illustrate how architectural professionals at that time promoted the views of the government while at the same time attempting to interpret such views based on their own understandings.[21] I do not attempt to give a total account of the arguments raised by the authors of these articles, but hope to highlight the way the articles registered debates on the terms used in the government's principles for architecture.

While propaganda writings in *Architectural Journal* attempted to analyze the meaning of the government's architectural principles, the primary aim of such writings was still to promote the principles themselves. In "A Discussion," Zhai explicitly states that the aim of his article is to criticize formalism and revivalism. In the early 1950s, architects who had studied abroad under the Beaux-Arts program were called upon to serve the PRC, and employed Beaux-Arts design methods to create a Chinese version of "socialist realism with national forms." This is reflected in the buildings of that time which have Chinese features, especially the curved roofs of traditional Chinese architecture.[22] In 1955, revivalism was condemned by the government, but no definitive meaning was given to the term "revivalism," leading to subsequent debates about the meanings of both "revivalism" and

---

19   Xue 2006, p.4
20   *Architectural Journal,* 1955(01), p.46 - 68

21   See note 74.
22   Zhu 2009, p.75

認同的人士（例如蘇聯政治家及哲學家）的意見，均被視為支持論點的重要論證。在《論建築藝術與美及民族形式》一文，翟立林直接援引馬克思及恩格斯的學說，支持「建築是一種藝術」的論點。此論點其實非常普遍，不過在毛澤東時期，如此明顯的論點似乎仍需得到社會主義政府的認可，才顯得有說服力。另外文中亦援引毛澤東的見解，支持中共需要一種新的民族形式此論點，而毛澤東的意見亦被形容為「英明的指示」。[27]在討論美學概念時，翟立林引用「十九世紀的偉大的俄國作家、科學美學的奠基人車爾尼雪夫斯基（Nikolai Chernyshevsky）」的見解，指出藝術的首要任務就是重現自然與生活，「任何東西，我們在那裡面看得見依照我們的概念應當如此的生活，那就是美的；任何東西，凡是獨自表現生活或使人憶起生活的，那就是美的。」[28]車爾尼雪夫斯基的美學概念被視為「偉大」，[29]在文中被視作美學的唯一概念，而通篇有關美學的討論均以此概念為根基。在政府宣傳性文章中，

蘇聯的哲學家及理念被經常援引，且被視作權威，不過資本主義國家的哲學家，包括普遍備受各界重視的美學權威康德 (Immanuel Kant) ，則幾乎未被援引。毛澤東時期的建築寫作反映了當時的作者採用了簡單的二分法，區分「資本主義」或「西方」國家的建築，以及「社會主義」國家的建築。這些文章直接使用「資本主義」、「西方」及「社會主義」這些字眼，區別不同建築。在本書中，這些字眼亦將在此建築層面上被理解。

於《建築學報》的宣傳性文章中，作者在探討建築創建方針所採用的字眼的意義時，往往採納一種分析性的論調，強調其論點的邏輯性，以表示他們是經過論證才支持政府提出的方針，而非盲從。在《論建築藝術與美及民族形式》一文，翟立林跟從政府的方向，批評形式主義和復古主義，提倡社會主義的建築應該具有「民族的形式，社會主義的內容。」[30]在批評「形式主義」和「復古主義」、提倡「民族形式」以前，翟立林嘗試定義這些字眼。他並

27　翟立林 1955, p.64
28　翟立林 1955, p.48
29　同上

30　翟立林 1955, p.60

"national form." Zhai stresses in the introduction to his article that it is based on various documents from architecture and construction conferences held in Russia and the PRC.[23] Throughout the article, the principles for architecture set by the government are either directly or indirectly reiterated. For example, Zhai writes that "the direction for development of our architectural profession must be based on the direction set by the government."[24] He states that the "functional, economical, and delightful if conditions permit" principle is "correct."[25] Zhai also points out that "architecture's function and technology are the most important and basic, while ideology is secondary and derivative."[26] This was another way to reiterate the principle that architecture should be "functional, economical, and delightful if conditions permit."

Government propaganda writings in *Architectural Journal* treat the views of CCP officials, especially Mao, and of figures recognized by the CCP, such as Russian politicians and philosophers, as significant or essential evidence to support the arguments of the authors. In "A Discussion," Zhai uses direct quotes from Karl Marx and Friedrich Engels to support the view that architecture is a form of art, as if this commonly-held view could only be valid if approved by the socialist government. Mao is quoted in support of the view that the PRC needs a new national form, a view Zhai describes as "luminous."[27] When discussing the concept of aesthetics, Zhai quotes the Russian critic and writer Nikolai Chernyshevsky, who believed that "the first purpose of art is to reproduce nature and life."[28] The concept of aesthetics articulated by Chernyshevsky, described as "magnificent"[29] in the article, is treated as the only definitive concept of aesthetics, and the subsequent part of the article is based on this concept. Unsurprisingly, while quotes from Russian philosophers and theorists were treated as authoritative in government propaganda writings, philosophers associated with capitalist countries, notably figures such as Immanuel Kant, were seldom, if ever, quoted. In architecture writings of the Maoist era, a simple dichotomy between the architecture of "capitalist," or "western," countries and the architecture of "socialist" countries was assumed. The labels "capitalist," "western" and "socialist" were directly employed as distinguishing terms in architecture writings, and in this book the terms are used in this specific context in relation to architecture.

23   Zhai 1955, p.46
24   Zhai 1955, p.66
25   Zhai 1955, p.67
26   Zhai 1955, p.53

27   Zhai 1955, p.64
28   Zhai 1955, p.48
29   Ibid.

未舉出個別建築物的實例來說明這些字眼，反以一個理論層面討論這些字眼的意思。在定義形式主義和復古主義時，翟立林分析了「建築的內容」，[31]亦即建築的功能、技術及美學之間的關係。翟立林得出的結論是中共需要「服從社會主義內容」的「新的民族形式」，而「民族形式」並非「把古老的民族形式照樣的搬用」，抄襲中國傳統建築。[32]在文中，「分析」、「研究」以及「辯證」等字眼經常出現，而翟立林亦強調文中的討論並無偏頗，敦促讀者理解其論證。例如在解釋功能與美學在建築中的關係時，翟立林說：「對於建築的功能和美觀問題，正像對於任何其他的問題一樣，必須歷史地、具體地加以考察而決定，不可一概而論。」[33]當翟立林嘗試定義「建築的內容」時，他先承認建築的內容「存在著多種不同的解釋」，再提出他對於建築的內容的定義：「功能、技術及思想性三者是統一地容納在一個建築形式之中的三種內容或內容的三種成分。」[34]《論建築藝術與美及民族形式》一文反映了在50年代中期，《建築學報》的政府宣傳性文章的作者，認同政府訂立的建築創建方針可以引

發不同釋義。建築專業人士似乎意識到方針所用字眼的釋義以及某種釋義的普遍性會影響大眾對方針的理解，而建築專業人士亦鼓勵就有關字眼的討論。

翟立林的文章定義了形式主義、復古主義及民族形式的意思，從而展開了一場有關這些字眼釋義的辯論。在1955至1957年間，《建築學報》刊登了回應《論建築藝術與美及民族形式》的不同文章。1955年，《建築學報》首先刊登了兩篇挑戰翟立林對於「建築的內容」的定義的文章，包括建築師閻家瑞撰寫的《對翟立林同志『論建築藝術的特徵』的幾點意見》，[35]以及當時中國人民大學建築系教授周祥源的《論建築藝術的內容 ── 與翟立林同志商榷》。[36]1956年，由清華大學的陳志華、英若聰撰寫的《評翟立林『論建築藝術與美及民族形式』》[37]在《建築學報》刊登。由於政府從未參與有關討論，為建築的創建方針提出一個「正確」的釋義，建築專業人士之間的討論因此可以繼續進行。

這些回應文章的作者都與翟立林一樣，認同形式主義及復古主義不應被鼓勵，亦有重申

31　翟立林 1955, p.53
32　翟立林 1955, p.63
33　翟立林 1955, p.47
34　翟立林 1955, p.53

35　《建築學報》，1955(03), p.96-97
36　《建築學報》，1955(03), p.98-100
37　《建築學報》，1956(02), p.1-11

Authors of propaganda writings in *Architectural Journal*, when exploring the meanings of terms used in the government's architectural principles, employed an analytical tone, emphasizing the logic of their arguments to suggest that their support for the government's principles was not merely based on blind conformity. In "A Discussion," Zhai, following the directions of the government, criticizes formalism and revivalism and promotes the principle that socialist architecture should have "socialist content with national form."[30] Zhai also tries to define the meanings of these terms. Rather than illustrating the meanings with specific architectural examples, however, he discusses them at a theoretical level. In defining formalism and revivalism, Zhai attempts to analyze the "content of architecture,"[31] or the relationship between function, technology and aesthetics. Zhai concludes that the PRC needs "a new national form" that reflects the conditions of socialist society, and that "a national form" was not one that copied traditional Chinese architecture.[32] Terms such as "analyze," "research," and "dialectical analysis" are used throughout the article. Zhai emphasizes that the discussion in the article is not biased, and he urges readers to attempt to understand his reasoning.

For example, when explaining the relationship between function and aesthetics in architecture, Zhai writes: "Like any other question, the question about the levels of importance of function and aesthetics should be considered in a concrete manner with reference to history, and we should not adopt a one-sided view."[33] When explaining what he means by the "content of architecture," Zhai recognizes that "there are many different interpretations about the content of architecture" before proposing his own definition — that the "content of architecture" includes the "function, technology, and ideology" of architecture.[34] As judged by the example of "A Discussion," government propaganda writings in *Architectural Journal* in the mid-1950s recognized that there were multifaceted interpretations of the architectural design and construction principles. Architectural professionals seemed to be aware that the connotations attached to different terms affected people's understanding of the principles, and they encouraged debates on the meanings of these terms.

Zhai's article, which attempted to define the meanings of formalism, revivalism and national form, led to a debate. Articles commenting on "A Discussion" appeared in *Architectural Journal* between

30   Zhai 1955, p.60
31   Zhai 1955, p.53
32   Zhai 1955, p.63

33   Zhai 1955, p.47
34   Zhai 1955, p.53

政府提出的建築創建方針，不過每個作者對於方針所運用的字眼都有不同詮釋。換言之，儘管幾個作者之間存有一定共識，認為形式主義及復古主義不應被鼓勵，他們仍就翟立林是否或如何理解形式主義及復古主義進行辯論，並爭辯甚麼才是反對形式主義及復古主義的「正確」論據。在這些文章中，作者在討論翟立林的論據時，通常使用到「正確」及「錯誤」這些字眼。

在《對翟立林同志『論建築藝術的特徵』的幾點意見》一文中，閻家瑞同意形式主義及復古主義不應被鼓勵，因為建築應該講求經濟，但他指翟立林為了強調節約的重要性，「不適當的舉出例子」。[38]在《評翟立林『論建築藝術與美及民族形式』》一文，陳志華及英若聰指「崔先生的錯誤還在於[建築的內容]這個問題的提法和敘述的方法上」。[39]1957年，《建築學報》刊登了翟立林對有關《論建築藝術與美及民族形式》的評論的回應，[40]翟立林主要攻擊陳

38 閻家瑞 1955, p.96
39 陳志華及英若聰 1956, p.5
40 《再論建築藝術與美及民族形式》，《建築學報》, 1957(01), p.39-48

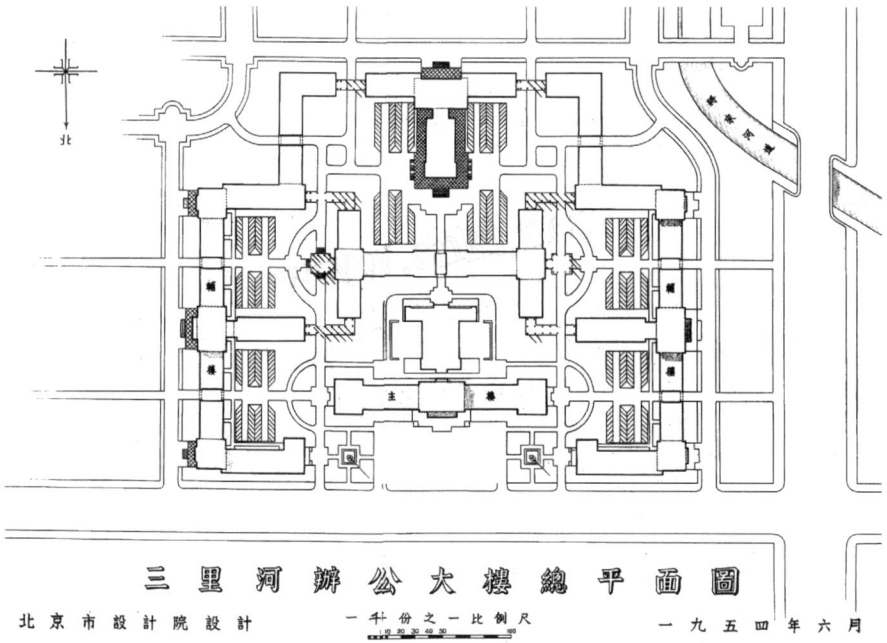

Plan, Sanlihe Office Building, Beijing, 1954
三里河辦公大樓平面圖，北京，1954年

三里河辦公大樓總平面圖

北京市設計院設計　　一千份之一比例尺　　一九五四年六月

1955 and 1957. The first two articles, challenging Zhai's definition of the "content of architecture," were published in 1955: "Some Comments on Mr. Zhai Lilin's 'A Discussion on the Characteristics of Architecture as Art'"[35] ("Some Comments") written by architect Yan Jiarui, and "A Discussion on the Content of Architecture as Art — Questioning Mr. Zhai Lilin"[36] ("Questioning Mr. Zhai Lilin") written by Zhou Xiangyuan, then architecture professor at Renmin University of China. In 1956, an article titled "A Criticism on Zhai Lilin's 'A Discussion on Architecture as Art in Relation to Aesthetics and National Form'"[37] ("A Criticism") written by Chen Zhihua and Ying Ruocong from Tsinghua University was published. The government did not participate in this debate to give the "correct" interpretations of the principles, which allowed the debate to carry on.

The authors of these articles agree with Zhai that formalism and revivalism should be discouraged, and they reiterate the principles for architecture design and construction set by the government. However, all the authors have their own interpretations of the terms used in the principles. In other words, although there was a consensus among the authors that formalism and revivalism should be

35　*Architectural Journal,* 1955(03), p.96-97
36　*Architectural Journal,* 1955(03), p.98-100
37　*Architectural Journal,* 1956(02), p.1-11

志華及英若聰文章的邏輯缺憾，指他自己在《論建築藝術與美及民族形式》一文中有關建築的內容的問題提法是否正確，「是另外一個問題」。[41]換言之，以《論建築藝術與美及民族形式》為中心的辯論停留在辯論技巧的層面，並未討論形式主義及復古主義本身是否應該備受抨擊。《建築學報》的文章反映了1978年以前，有關建築創建方針的辯論並非旨在挑戰方針的適用性，而這些辯論只是以不同的論證手法引證政府的方針的合理性。

起初回應翟立林《論建築藝術與美及民族形式》一文的文章，都是比較溫和的批評，及後刊登的文章則採用更具批判性的論調。《對翟立林同志『論建築藝術的特徵』的幾點意見》及《論建築藝術的內容 — 與翟立林同志商榷》兩篇文章的語調都非常客氣，作者在文中都表示贊同翟立林與政府一致的立場。例如在《對翟立林同志『論建築藝術的特徵』的幾點意見》一文，閻家瑞在文章開始說：「我認為[翟立林同志的]文章在某些小的地方語氣還不夠完整，特別提出來希望翟立林同志指正」，[42]開首就為文章訂立溫和的論調。在《論建築藝術

41　翟立林 1957, p.40
42　閻家瑞 1955, p.96

discouraged, there was a debate about the "correct" way of arguing against formalism and revivalism, and whether Zhai had "correctly" understood these terms. All the authors frequently use the terms "right" and "wrong" when describing the arguments made by Zhai in "A Discussion."

In "Some Comments," Yan agrees with Zhai's view that formalism and revivalism should be discouraged because architecture should be economical, but he challenges Zhai for "emphasizing such a view with an inappropriate example."[38] In "A Criticism," Chen and Ying point out that "Zhai's mistakes lie in the way he approaches the problem [of the 'content of architecture.']"[39] Zhai's response to these criticisms, published in 1957,[40] attacks flaws in the logic of the article by Chen and Ying, saying that "whether his [own] views [on the 'content of architecture'] are correct or not is another question."[41] In other words, the focus of the debate about "A Discussion" remains restricted to the techniques of argument, while taking for granted that formalism and revivalism should be discouraged.

Perspective, Sanlihe Office Building, Beijing, 1954
三里河辦公大樓透視圖，北京，1954年

38 Yan 1955, p.96
39 Chen and Ying 1956, p.5
40 "Another Discussion on Architecture as Art in Relation to Aesthetics and National Form," *Architectural Journal,* 1957(01), p.39-48
41 Zhai 1957, p.40

的內容 ── 與翟立林同志商榷》一文，周祥源在通篇都稱呼翟立林為「立林同志」，彷彿將翟立林視作友好的同儕，減低了文章論調的批判性。閻家瑞及周祥源在挑戰翟立林對於「建築的內容」的見解時，均先在文中強調翟立林的一些見解「是完全正確的」。例如在《論建築藝術的內容 ── 與翟立林同志商榷》一文，周祥源在文章開首說：「作者試圖用馬克思主義辯證唯物論的哲學原理來分析有關建築的若干基本問題，有許多論點是正確的」，接著他便舉出例子，說明翟立林的部分論點「正確」。[43]相反地，《評翟立林『論建築藝術與美及民族形式』》一文採納了一種非常具批判性的論調。文章指出翟立林《論建築藝術與美及民族形式》一文提出的論點，與他聲稱反對形式主義的立場相矛盾，該文因此與政府訂立的建築創建方針相悖。在文章開首，陳志華及英若聰就指出翟立林「在研究理論中脫離了建築的社會實踐，只是從一些教條和概念出發，因此造成許多錯誤」，並表明他們會在文中「提出翟立林先生的一些明顯錯誤」。[44]在通篇文章，二人確實不斷指出翟立林的「錯誤」，強調「如

43　周祥源 1955, p.98
44　陳志華及英若聰 1956, p.1

Debates registered by writings in *Architectural Journal* before 1978 did not question the government's principles for architecture, but instead tried to justify them with different paths of reasoning.

The earlier responses to Zhai's article are milder criticisms, while those that appear later have a more critical tone. Both "Some Comments" and "Questioning Mr. Zhai Lilin" have a respectful tone and approve of Zhai's overall stance, which was aligned with that of the government. For example, in "Some Comments," Yan sets a moderate tone by saying at the beginning that "I feel that there are certain points in [Zhai's] article that have not been fully developed, so I will point these out and I hope that Mr. Zhai Lilin will correct me if I am wrong."[42] Zhou calls Zhai by his first name throughout "Questioning Mr. Zhai Lilin," making the article seem less critical. In both Yan's and Zhou's articles, before challenging Zhai's views about the "content of architecture," the authors emphasize that some of Zhai's views are "absolutely correct." In "Questioning Mr. Zhai Lilin," Zhou asserts in the introduction that "many of [Zhai's] arguments were correct" and gives examples of them.[43] In contrast, "A Criticism" has a much more critical tone. It asserts that Zhai's article did not actually condemn formalism, as he claimed, and that "A Discussion" thus contradicted the government's principles for architectural production. At the beginning of the article, Chen and Ying say that Zhai made a lot of "obvious mistakes,"[44] and Zhai's "mistakes" are pointed out throughout the article. Chen and Ying stress that "if Zhai had based his article on the policies of the Party, he would not have made so many mistakes."[45] These articles show two features of the debate about the principles for architecture design and construction in the 1950s: first, that some architectural professionals had a tinge of reluctance about criticizing their peers and this attitude might have limited the expression of opposing views; second, despite this reluctance to criticize, articles deemed to contradict the architectural principles set by the government could nevertheless meet harsh condemnation. Government authority in the realm of architecture could not be challenged.

The articles on "A Discussion" also reflect a debate about the importance of theory in discussions concerning the principles for architecture. While Zhai's analysis of formalism and revivalism is theoretical, Chen and Ying base their discussion on "common sense," expressing the view that the

42   Yan 1955, p.96
43   Zhou 1955, p.98
44   Chen and Ying 1956, p.1
45   Chen and Ying 1956, p.10

果翟先生在他的整個論文中，都能以黨的政策作為理論結論的準繩，那就不致於弄得錯誤百出了。」[45]這些文章反映了50年代關於建築創建方針的辯論的兩項特徵：第一，部分建築專業人士不願意批評業內夥伴，而這種態度大有可能限制了他們在辯論中提出反對意見。第二，儘管作者大多不願意批評他人，但被視為與政府提出的建築創建方針稍有相悖的文章都被猛烈批評。這是因為毛澤東時期的政府在建築創建上掌握所有權力，不可能被挑戰。環繞《論建築藝術與美及民族形式》的文章反映了在有關建築創建方針的討論中，建築專業人士對理論的重要性並未存有共識。翟立林有關形式主義及復古主義的討論較為理論化，陳志華及英若聰的討論則基於「一般常識」，他們指出翟立林在《論建築藝術與美及民族形式》一文的「錯誤」是「由於他在研究理論中脫離了建築的社會實踐」。[46]他們相信「研究今天的建築理論問題，應該找出建築的本質特徵。但這本質特徵絕不能僅以建築的本身去探求；也就是

絕不能脫離開建築的社會條件和經濟條件，脫離開建築為誰服務這個最根本的問題。」[47]他們認為基於「複雜的哲學問題」的討論，往往「違反了常識」。[48]二人亦指出「對建築不作與社會相聯繫的具體分析，而僅僅從內容與形式相統一這個一般原理出發，是不會得出很有用的結論來的。」[49]雖然二人並未明確定義甚麼是「有用」的討論，但從文中，可以知道二人所指「有用」的討論，等同有關如何令設計「實用、經濟、在可能條件下注意美觀」的討論。陳志華及英若聰就有關理論的討論，引發建築師袁祖德撰寫於1957年在《建築學報》刊登的《在論『建築藝術與美及民族形式』討論中和陳、英兩先生的不同意見》。[50]在文中，袁祖德提出理論的重要性，指出「今天我們如果不從理論上徹底清算形式主義，不樹立一些基本觀念的話，要真正使建築健康發展是很難想像的。」[51]總的來說，在1978年以前，建築的實際建造似乎比建築理論重要得多，在有關建築創建方針的討論中，理論並非必要的支持論據，

45　陳志華及英若聰 1956, p.10
46　陳志華及英若聰 1956, p.1

47　陳志華及英若聰 1956, p.2
48　陳志華及英若聰 1956, p.4
49　陳志華及英若聰 1956, p.7-8
50　《建築學報》，1957(01), p.61-63
51　袁祖德 1957, p.61

"mistakes" in "A Discussion" resulted because Zhai's focus on theory left him detached from the reality of society.[46] They argue that discussions on architectural principles should not be separated from social and economic conditions,[47] and that "complicated philosophical problems" often contradict "common sense."[48] They further point out that an emphasis on theories makes discussions about architecture generic and not very useful.[49] Here the authors did not explicitly define the meaning of "useful," but from the article, it is fair to assume that the authors consider discussions on how to make designs "functional, economical, and delightful if conditions permit" as "useful" discussions. Chen's and Ying's views on theory led architect Yuan Zude to write an article titled "Concerning the Discussion About 'A Discussion on Architecture as Art in Relation to Aesthetics and National Form' — My Views that Differ from Those of Mr. Chen and Mr. Ying" published in 1957.[50] In the article, Yuan upholds the importance of theory, saying that "if we do not analyze formalism on a theoretical level and set up the basic principles [for architecture design and construction], healthy architectural development would be beyond imagination."[51] Overall, however, it seems that in the pre-1978 era, the actual production of buildings was much more important than theories of architecture. Theory was not seen as essential in informing debates on the principles for architecture, and was even seen as an obstacle by some architectural professionals. This attitude hindered discussions about the relationship between theories and the material reality of architectural design and construction.

Government Propaganda and the Practice of Architecture

Government propaganda writings reflected the government manipulation of architectural design and construction in the Maoist era. With a "proletarian dictatorship" under the CCP, national goals for architecture design and construction were set by the state and design tasks were assigned through the

46   Chen and Ying 1956, p.1
47   Chen and Ying 1956, p.2
48   Chen and Ying 1956, p.4
49   Chen and Ying 1956, p.7-8
50   *Architectural Journal*, 1957(01), p.61-63

51   Yuan 1957, p.61

甚至被某些建築專業人士視為障礙。這種態度妨礙了他們討論理論與建築實質創建之間的關係。

政府宣傳與建築實踐

政府宣傳性文章反映了毛澤東時期，政府操控了建築創建。當時中共實行「無產階級專政」，政府就建築創建訂立全國性目標，而設計工作則經由國家的經濟及發展計劃分配。[52]至1953年，所有於1949年以前成立的私營建築公司均收歸國有，成為政府擁有的設計所；所有建築師隸屬一個特定的設計所，而他們都沒有空間實現自己或其專業的自主性，進行思考或設計。[53]由於政府掌握了所有土地及建築建設的資源，建築師不能挑戰政府訂立的建築創建方針，只能跟從政府的指示。

有關建築創建方針所用字眼的討論，反映自1949年，建築師都在為當代中國尋求新的民族形式。這些建築師過去曾於「舊中國」執業，當中大部分於20年代在國外接受過巴黎美術院派（Beaux-Arts）課程教育，[54]他們將自己的技術及知識運用在代表新中國的政治任務上。[55]在50年代初蘇聯「社會現實主義」的影響下，包含巴黎美術院派折衷主義元素的復古建築一度在國盛行，相反，被視為象徵資本主義的當代主義建築則備受批評。在1955年節約政策之下，社會現實主義建築的實驗一度暫停，擁有大屋頂及傳統裝飾的建築物均被視為浪費，而當代主義建築則被視為同樣適合資本主義及社會主義國家。[56]1959年，亦即中華人民共和國成立十周年，毛澤東政府提出興建「民族形式，社會主義內容」的建築，社會現實主義於是再度盛行。這段時期的建築表彰民族主義，有明確的中國特色，當中以國慶十大工程為代表的建築更充滿了巴黎美術院派的裝飾性色彩，採用中國式的細部及中國式的屋頂，抗衡被視作

52　Xue 2006, p.157
53　Zhu 2009, p.103

54　Zhu 2009, p.75
55　同上
56　Lu 2006, p.121

country's economic and development plan.[52] By 1953, all private architectural firms established before 1949 had been grouped into public companies and then into state-owned design institutes. Every architect belonged to a particular design institute, and architectural professionals had no room to act with individual or professional autonomy.[53] Architects could not challenge the architectural principles set by the government but were compelled to follow these principles, as the government controlled all the land and resources for architectural development.

The debates over the meanings of terms in these architectural principles registered the search by architects for "a national style for a modern nation-state in China" that had begun in 1949. Most of these architects had practiced in the "Old China" and had studied abroad in a Beaux-Arts program in the 1920s.[54] They were "offering their skills and knowledge for the political task of representing the new Republic."[55] In the early 1950s, revivalist architecture containing elements of Beaux-Arts eclecticism was dominant under the influence of the Soviet ideal of "Socialist Realism," while the modernist style, considered capitalist, fell into disrepute. With the advent of the austerity policy of 1955, experimentation with Socialist Realist architecture was suspended. Buildings with large roofs and traditional ornaments were condemned as wasteful, and modernist architecture came to be considered suitable for both capitalist and socialist countries.[56] In 1959, ten years after the establishment of the PRC, there was a second wave of "Socialist Realism" under the principle of creating "socialist content with national form" upheld by the Maoist government. A national style with tangible Chinese features, as exemplified by the Ten Grand Buildings designed in a decorative Beaux-Arts language with literal Chinese details and Chinese roofs, was adopted. This Chinese national style was presented in opposition to modernism and the International Style, which were once again condemned as aesthetic instruments of capitalist imperialism.[57] In the 1960s and 1970s, the more economical socialist functionalism gradually dominated the country.[58] As the changing styles of buildings reflects, the idea of "a new socialist architectural style in China" was open for interpretation

52   Xue 2006, p.157
53   Zhu 2009, p.103
54   Zhu 2009, p.75
55   Ibid.

56   Lu 2006, p.121
57   Zhu 2009, p.213
58   Zhu 2009, p.106

Beijing Railway Station, one of the Ten Grand Buildings, 1959
北京火車站，國慶十大工程之一，1959年

Beijing Workers' Stadium, one of the Ten Grand Buildings, 1959
北京工人體育場，國慶十大工程之一，1959年

資本帝國主義美學工具的當代主義建築及國際主義建築。[57] 在1960至1970年代，建造成本較低的社會實用主義建築漸漸風行全國。[58]從建築物不斷轉變的風格可見，「新的社會主義建築風格」這個概念，自1949年以至1980年代一直未有明確的定義，而自1980年代開始，中國的建築界開始要求多元化，以「時代特色，民族特色，地方特色」取代「社會主義內容，民族形式」。[59]

政府宣傳性文章是毛澤東時期一種獨特的寫作，反映了政府操控有關建築創建方針的論述。政府將自己塑造成「公共利益」的代表，聲稱其意見代表了大眾的意見。政府宣傳性文章並非旨在引起大眾對建築創建方針的辯論，卻用作促使大眾支持有關方針。不過，建築專業人士自發性地展開了有關建築創建方針所使用的字眼的辯論，抓緊機會挑戰及詮釋方針，企圖影響建築創建。

57   Zhu 2009, p.213
58   Zhu 2009, p.106
59   Xue 2006, p.7

from 1949 until the 1980s, when Chinese architectural circles started to appeal for pluralism, replacing "socialist content, national form" with "features of times, nationality, regionalism."[59]

Propaganda writings also reflected the government's manipulation of the discourse on architectural principles. The state established itself as a representative of the "public interest," claiming that government opinions represented those of the general public. Propaganda writings did not aim to open up the principles for debate but urged the audience to support the principles. However, as architectural professionals engaged in debate over the terms used in the principles, they attempted to seize the chance to influence architecture design and construction by introducing their own interpretations.

59   Xue 2006, p.7

An education institute in Henan, typical economical design, 1970s
河南一所師範教學樓，展示社會實用主義的建築，1970年代

(above) Plan, an education institute in Henan, 1970s
（上）河南一所師範教學樓平面圖，1970年代

(below) Detail, an education institute in Henan, 1970s
（下）河南一所師範教學樓建築細部，1970年代

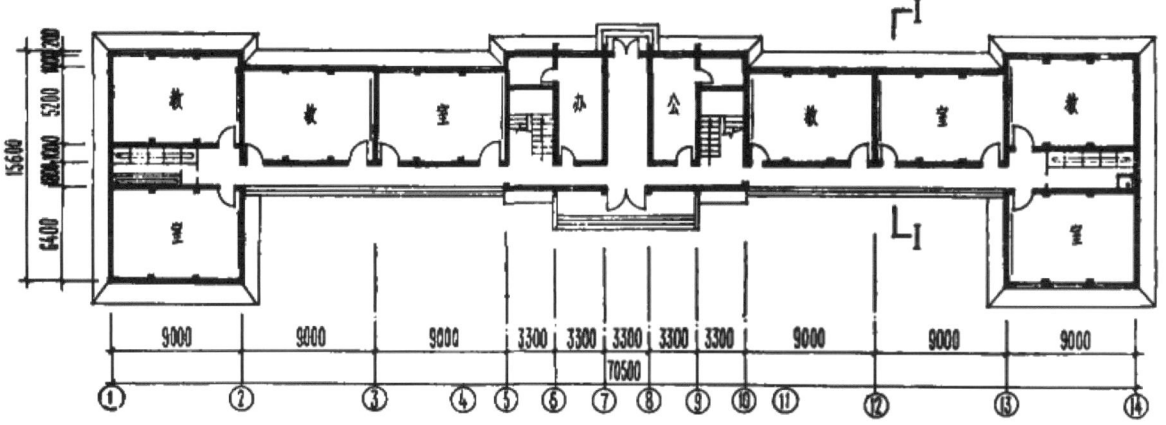

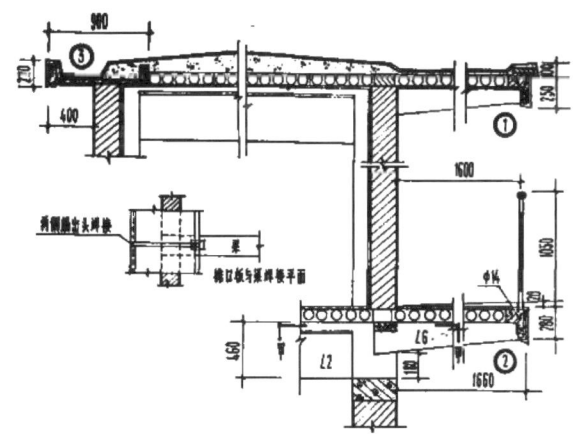

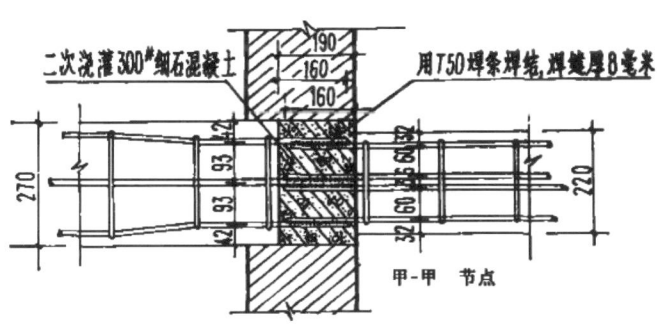

二次澆灌300#細石混凝土　　　用T50焊條焊結,焊縫厚8毫米

甲-甲　节点

INTRODUCTORY ARTICLES: WRITING TO "INFORM"

Introductory articles in the mass media give information about important or interesting new buildings or architectural practices, while those in field journals also provide technical information for the use of those working in the building industry. Introductory articles do not aim to make explicit judgments about the buildings discussed, though they often carry implicit evaluations of such buildings. The introductory articles reviewed in this book include articles written by reporters and architectural professionals, interviews with architects which give facts about a building or explain the design intent, and profile stories on architects.

Introductory Articles in Newspapers

As an alternative to promoting its architectural principles directly through propaganda writings, introductory articles in newspapers provided the Maoist government with a more subtle way to advocate its views. Only buildings that exemplified the principles set by the government were written about in newspapers. Appreciation was expressed through the choices of the buildings that writers took seriously enough to introduce, and the buildings introduced were all associated with positive notions. Most introductory articles in newspapers were written by architects or reporters

介紹性文章：以文字「告知」

　　大眾傳媒的介紹性文章介紹重要或有趣的新建築，或提供有關建築界的資訊，而專業期刊的文章也會向業界提供技術資訊。介紹性文章並不旨在對所介紹的建築物進行明確的批判，但通常在討論中，作者都會反映出對建築物不言明的評價。本書討論的介紹性文章包括由記者及建築專業人士撰寫的文章及建築師的訪問，這些文章提供建築師設計的作品資訊，或解釋其設計動機；本書亦會討論建築師的人物特寫。

報章的介紹性文章

　　毛澤東政府除了以宣傳性文章直接宣揚建築創建方針外，亦透過介紹性文章，以一個較低調的方法提倡政府的意見，故當時只有能彰顯政府訂立的建築創建方針的建築物，才會被報章介紹。作者選擇他們認為值得介紹的建築物，而這已反映出他們欣賞該建築物，故此類介紹性文章均內容正面。報章的介紹性文章主要由建築師或記者撰寫，介紹在中國或其他社會主義國家由集體創作產生的經濟、實用的建築物。

and introduced economical and functional buildings designed collectively in China or other socialist countries.

Introductory articles written by architects often emphasized the organizational identity of the architects. Organizational identity traditionally serves as a collective framework for members to take action, and to make sense of their world.[60] In this case, organizational identity refers to the shared beliefs of architects about their profession, which was then controlled by the Maoist government. The first-person plural "we," instead of the first-person singular "I," was used in these articles. Articles seldom mentioned the name of any individual architect. For example, "We Designed Classrooms that are Economical and Functional" ("We Designed Classrooms"), published in *People's Daily* on 27 August 1955, uses the byline "Shandong Province Architecture and Construction Studio," which was a group of architects working under the government. The first-person plural, "we," is used throughout the article in explaining the department's work. The article contains sentences like "We set the budget for the project;" "We tried to make the design simple and functional;" and "We as the designers of architecture feel that there is still room to lower the costs of construction." Another article, "We Have

Made New Standard Designs" ("Standard Designs"), written by architect Yan Zixiang of the Ministry of Construction and published on 18 September 1955 in *People's Daily*, emphasizes that the standard designs introduced were made by "us — the design department of the Ministry of Construction." In other words, introductory articles written by architects of the Maoist era emphasized collective effort, and individual architects were discouraged from taking credit for designs.

Such articles also emphasized how the buildings introduced complied with the principles for architecture design and construction set by the government, in particular the principle that buildings should be economical. In contrast, function and aesthetics were treated as less significant. The article "Standard Designs" details the costs of constructing buildings according to standard designs, and different aspects of the standard designs are described in relation to costs. For example, Yan says the average life cycle of buildings built with standard designs is 50 to 80 years, and "the cheapest bungalow can last for ten to 15 years." He also says the choice of building materials should depend on material costs, which comprise "70 percent of the total construction costs."

The articles were structured so that functional aspects of buildings were introduced only after

60   Golden-Biddle and Rao 1997, p.594

建築師撰寫的介紹性文章通常強調建築師的組織身份。組織身份是指一個組織成員對其組織長期建立的核心特質的信仰。這種信仰為成員提供一個整體框架，有助他們理解世界，以及思考行動。[60]在這裡，組織身份是指建築師對於其專業的共同信仰，而有關信仰卻被毛澤東政府操控。建築師撰寫的介紹性文章通常不採用第一人稱的單數「我」，而採用第一人稱的複數「我們」，而某特定建築師的名字很少會被提及。例如1955年8月27日於《人民日報》刊登的《我們設計了既經濟又適用的教室》，文章的署名是山東省建築工程設計室，是政府轄下的建築師組織。通篇文章在介紹設計室的工作時，均使用了第一人稱複數「我們」，例如：「根據我們編制的工程預算」、「我們力求做到簡單、適用」、「我們做設計工作的同志，都感到還有進一步降低造價的潛力」等。1955年9月18日於《人民日報》刊登的《我們完成了新的標準設計》由建築工程部部長閻子祥撰寫，文章開首就強調「最近，我們 ─ 建築工程部設計總局根據中央提出的非生產性建築造價指標，完成了樓房的家屬住宅、單身宿舍、辦公室和平房的住宅、宿舍、辦公室等六類民用建築的設計。」換言之，在毛澤東時期，由建築師撰寫的介紹性文章都強調集體創作，而個別建築師對設計的個人貢獻則備受忽略。

此類由建築師撰寫的介紹性文章亦強調所介紹的建築物如何符合政府訂立的建築創建方針，尤其是建築物應該講求經濟這項原則。相反地，實用性和美學並未得到相應重視。《我們完成了新的標準設計》一文列出了採用標準設計的建築物的造價，而文中就標準設計的討論均與造價有關。例如閻子祥指出以標準設計建造的「樓房可以保證使用五十到八十年，最便宜的平房可以保證使用十年到十五年，磚木結構的平房可以使用二十到四十年。」他又指建築物的材料選擇繫於材料價格，「建築材料一般佔全部建築造價的百分之七十」。由文章的結構所見，作者往往在確定一所建築物講求經濟原則以後，才開始討論建築物的實用性。在討論如何顧及建築物的實用性時，建築師通常使用「盡量」這個字眼，顯示建築師只能在講求經濟的前提下，盡量改善建築物的質素；換言之，講求經濟是最重要的建築創建方針，

60 Golden-Biddle and Rao 1997, p.594

it was made clear that the buildings were economical. When describing how to make buildings functional, the architects used terms such as "try the utmost," suggesting they could merely do their best under the overriding principle of economical construction. For example, in "Standard Design," Yan says architects "gave as much consideration as they could to the functional requirements of the buildings," and they "tried their utmost" to ensure that all the rooms in the dormitories and residential buildings faced a desirable direction. Yan also admits in the article that standard designs undermined functional and aesthetic aspects — standard designs had "monotonous façades that did not fulfil the aesthetic requirements well," and "there had not been enough consideration given to the functional needs of the buildings." The article "We Designed Classrooms" further exemplifies the high priority given to reducing costs. A large part of the article is dedicated to describing how the architects tried to lower construction costs by using concrete reinforced with bamboo instead of steel, reducing the snow load-bearing capacity of the buildings from 50kg to 20kg; by designing classrooms with the same size; and so on. The article states towards the end that the classrooms, while having low construction costs, could nevertheless "completely satisfy the needs of the students." However, this seems more a defense against possible accusations that function and aesthetics were sacrificed to reduce costs than a recognition of their importance.

"Fangua Nong Residential Design is Relatively Practical," *Wenhui Bao*, 10 April 1964
《蕃瓜弄住宅設計做到比較切合實際》，
《文匯報》，1964年4月10日

Fangua Nong Residential Area, Shanghai, 1960s
蕃瓜弄住宅，上海，1960年代

但講求經濟的原則同時亦對當時的建築創建施加了最大掣肘。例如在《我們完成了新的標準設計》一文，閻子祥指出設計團隊在降低造價以外，「也最大限度地考慮了日常使用上的各種要求」，在宿舍和住宅的設計中，盡量使主要房間朝著好的方向。閻子祥承認，標準設計忽視了實用性及美觀，指出標準設計的建築物「體型立面又很單調，在佈置上不能適當照顧美觀要求」，而「對於居住的適用及部分技術措施，還有考慮不周的地方。」另外《我們設計了既經濟又適用的教室》一文，進一步顯示了降低成本的重要性。文中大部分內容都在形容建築師降低成本的方法，包括使用竹筋代替部分鋼筋來製造屋梁、將雪荷重計算標準由五十公斤降至二十公斤、使教室樓「每個房間的大小、規格盡可能相同」等。該文末段指出教室樓雖然成本下降，卻「完全適合學生的學習需要」。不過，此說法似乎旨在避免批評者指控建築師為降低成本而犧牲實用性及美觀，而非真正為了肯定實用性及美觀相對經濟而言的重要性。

　　相反地，由記者撰寫的介紹性文章則較為重視建築物的實用性。1954年6月20日於《人民日報》刊登的《首都劇場開工興建》一文，詳盡介紹了劇場不同部分的功能，解釋了舞台設

Introductory articles written by reporters, on the other hand, focused more attention on the function of buildings. "Capital Theater Construction Commences," ("Capital Theater") published in *People's Daily* on 20 June 1954, describes the function of different parts of the Theater in detail, explaining how the stage design facilitates set changes, and how the circulation design enables the audience to "leave the Theater within five minutes." In "Fangua Nong Residential Design is Relatively Practical," published in *Wenhui Bao* on 10 April 1964, the relationship between the design of Fangua Nong, a typical squatter settlement in Shanghai in the 1960s, and its users is emphasized. The article describes how the architects visited old Linongs[61] and organized research, interviews, and forums to make in-depth studies of the residents' requirements before developing the design. To illustrate how seriously the architects took the opinions of users, the article notes that the design had been changed 29 times based on the studies of users' requirements. Architects and reporters thus differed in the views they expressed in their introductory articles about whether cost or function was more important.

Communist Party of the Soviet Union Periphery Committee Building, Krasnoyarsk Krai, example of buildings introduced in *Architectural Journal* in the 1950s
蘇聯共產黨邊區委員會大樓，克拉斯諾特，《建築學報》在1950年代介紹的建築例子

Soviet Building, Pskov
蘇維埃大廈，普斯科夫

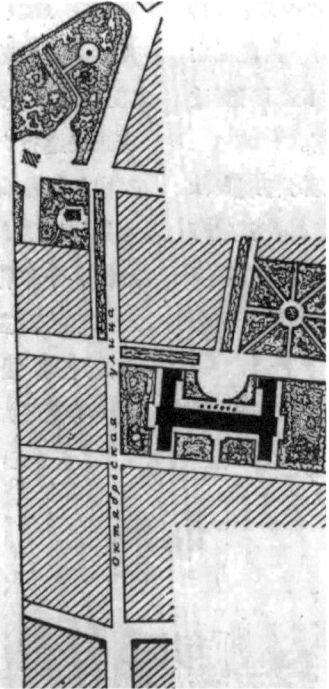

Overall plan, Soviet Building, Pskov, example of buildings introduced in *Architectural Journal* in the 1950s
蘇維埃大廈總平面圖，普斯科夫，
《建築學報》在1950年代介紹的建築例子

61   Linongs are traditional residential clusters with a very high density commonly found in Shanghai.

計如何有助更換佈景、動線設計如何在散場後於五分鐘內疏散觀眾等。1964年4月10日於《文匯報》刊登的《蕃瓜弄住宅設計做到比較切合實際》一文，強調了於1960年代於上海普遍出現的棚戶區之一 — 蕃瓜弄與居民之間的關係；文中形容建築師在設計前「深入實際，深入群眾，進行廣泛的調查研究」，到棚戶區和舊式里弄[61]調查、訪問、並召開座談會，理解居民的需要。為表示設計人員對居民意見的重視，文中提到「在調查研究的基礎上，設計人員共起草了二十九次規劃設計方案」。分別由建築師及記者撰寫的介紹性文章，顯示了他們對於成本和功能重要性存有不同理解。

《建築學報》的介紹性文章

1978年以前，《建築學報》的介紹性文章主要關於由中國及其他社會主義國家建築師所設計的建築物。在1954年的《建築學報》中，一半的內容都是關於蘇聯及東歐的建築與都市規劃。[62] 有關中國建築物的介紹性文章旨在展開有關本地設計的討論，在1954年第二期《建築學報》的〈編者的話〉一欄，作者明確指出「本期加了人民來信 — 批評與建設一欄，從人民日報社轉來了一篇林凡同志的來稿，人民對於我們建築工作是十分關懷的，要求我們改進建築工作的心情是十分誠懇迫切的，我們非常歡迎這類來稿，開展批評與自我批評，是提高我們建築事業的重要武器。」[63] 由於介紹性文章旨在開展有關建築的討論，《建築學報》介紹的設計並非一面倒的受讚賞，卻帶來討論空間。不過在1960年代文化大革命期間，《建築學報》似乎只會介紹表彰政府訂立的建築創建方針的建築物。《建築學報》的介紹性文章集中討論設計動機，並提供較技術性的設計及建造資訊。這類文章通常由被介紹的建築物的設計者撰寫，可以是一組建築師或代表整個團隊的個別建築師。

《建築學報》的介紹性文章為建築師提供參考指引，詳細描述建築物的整體佈局以至建築細部。為便於參考，文章往往清晰地分成不同部分，介紹建築物設計的不同方面。例如在

61　里弄是中國傳統住宅群的一種，密度非常高，在上海尤為普遍。

62　Lu 2006, p.312
63　《建築學報》，1954(02), p.125

Introductory Articles in *Architectural Journal*

Introductory articles in *Architectural Journal* before 1978 included articles on buildings designed by architects in other socialist countries as well as China. Half of the articles in *Architectural Journal* in 1954 were about architecture and urban planning in the Soviet Union and Eastern Europe.[62] Introductory articles on buildings in China aimed to launch discussions on local designs. The second issue of the journal invited comments on the buildings introduced.[63] As a result, designs were not necessarily portrayed as positive examples, but were open for debate. However, as the Cultural Revolution approached in the 1960s, the journal began to write only about buildings exemplifying the principles for architecture set by the government. Introductory articles in *Architectural Journal* focused on design intent and provided relatively more technical information on design and construction. They were written by groups of architects or individuals who represented the group responsible for the designs introduced.

Buildings introduced in *Architectural Journal*'s introductory articles were intended to serve as references for designs that architects could use. The articles thus gave detailed descriptions of the buildings, from overall organization to construction details. For easy reference, articles were clearly divided into different sections to introduce different aspects of the design. For example, "A Certain Hotel in the Western Suburbs of Beijing,"[64] ("A Certain Hotel"), written by Zhang Bo of Beijing Institute of Architectural Design and published in 1954, is divided into sections such as "overall organization," "plans," "facades," "construction materials," "structural organization," "building services," and so on. Facts and information are given in each section, providing a basis for readers to analyze and comment on the design. Although this article does not mention the name of the building, it gives the location of the building and includes its design drawings. Readers could thus easily identify the building and comment on it. In 1955, "The Extravagant Yet Impractical Hotel in the Western Suburbs,"[65] a commentary on the design of the hotel, was published (this article will be discussed later in the book). "An Introduction of the Design Scheme for the Grand Theater,"[66] ("An Introduction"), written by the Theater Design Group of the Department of Architecture of Tsinghua University and published

---

62   Lu 2006, p.31
63   *Architectural Journal,* 1954(02), p.125

64   *Architectural Journal,* 1954(01), p.40-41.
65   *Architectural Journal,* 1955(01), p.38-41
66   *Architectural Journal,* 1960(05), p.11-15.

1954年出版，由北京建築設計院張鎛撰寫的《北京西郊某招待所設計介紹》[64]一文，張鎛將文章分成「總體佈置」、「建築平面佈置」、「建築立面處理」、「建築內部用料」、「結構佈置」、「水暖佈置」、「電器佈置」等不同部分，並於各部分提供相關資訊，這些資訊成為讀者分析與評價建築設計的基礎。雖然這篇文章並未顯示被評論的建築物的名稱，但文中指出了建築物的地點，並刊載了其制圖，讀者因此可以辨認出該大樓，並作出評價。1955年，評論招待所的《華而不實的西郊招待所》[65]一文出版，本書稍後部分會詳細討論這篇文章。另外，1960年出版，由清華大學建築系劇院設計組撰寫的《大劇院設計方案介紹》[66]一文，則與《北京西郊某招待所設計介紹》一文不同，並未以相對中立的態度陳述有關劇院的資訊。在該文中，形容大劇院的文字多帶正面意思，如「大劇院將是這些代表著我們時代的雄偉而壯麗的人民宮殿中的一座」、「建築構築佈局採用了層次較多而又不封閉、豐富而又

有變化的處理手法」、「廁所的位置既隱蔽而又方便」等。這類文化大革命逼近期間出版的文章並非旨在提供有關建築物的資訊，反而意在影響讀者的意見，令讀者贊同根據政府訂立的建築創建方針建造的建築物都是好建築。

與由記者撰寫、在報章刊登的介紹性文章一樣，《建築學報》的介紹性文章強調建築物的功能性，但有關討論更專注技術層面以及探討建築物的美觀性。《大劇院設計方案介紹》一文提及「今天人民要求建築藝術的新風格應當反映我們國家社會主義蓬勃發展的現實，這樣一種風格，必然不同於古代的風格，也不同於資本主義世界的風格」，[67]陳述了有關大劇院的美學考慮。在這篇文章，「創造」一詞不斷出現，強調建築師嘗試建立的「社會主義新風格」是嶄新的，不過同時，在形容「社會主義新風格」時，作者亦經常提及中國傳統建築元素。在《北京西郊某招待所設計介紹》一文，作者指立面的「整個整體，採取重點的用大屋

64　《建築學報》，1954(01), p.40-41
65　《建築學報》，1955(01), p.38-41
66　《建築學報》，1960(05), p.11-15

67　清華大學建築系劇院設計組1960, P.15

in 1960, does not describe the building in the relatively neutral manner of "A Certain Hotel," but instead uses terms with positive meanings, such as "magnificent," "convenient," and "lively." As the Cultural Revolution approached, such articles did not merely aim to provide information about the building, but also to shape the audience's opinions, and to convince readers that buildings constructed according to the government's architectural principles were good buildings.

Similar to newspaper introductory articles written by reporters, introductory articles in *Architectural Journal* highlighted the functional aspects of buildings, though in more technical terms; at the same time, they also described the aesthetics of buildings. In "An Introduction," the "new" national style of architecture, "different from the traditional style and the style of the capitalist world,"[67] is described in terms of its aesthetic aspects. The word "create" is used incessantly to emphasize that the national style that architects were trying to shape is something "new." However, at the same time, terms denoting elements in traditional Chinese architecture are often used in descriptions of the "new" national style. In "A Certain Hotel," the "double eave roof" is described as the major element of the façade. The article also describes the use of "jishou," or mythical creatures, on flying eaves. In both "A

67   Theater Design Group, Tsinghua University 1960, P.15

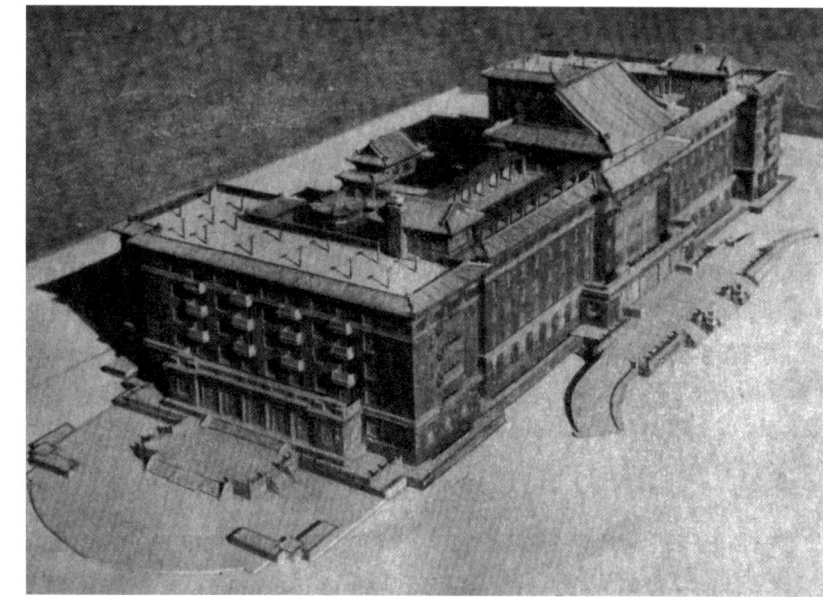

Perspective, A Certain Hotel in the Western Suburbs of Beijing, 1954
北京西郊某招待所透視圖，1954年

"Jishou," or mythical creatures, on flying eaves, A Certain
Hotel in the Western Suburbs of Beijing, 1954
北京西郊某招待所的「脊獸」，1954年

頂、亭子、小瓦檐及台基台子使整個輪廓線，在簡單的大塊邊沿上，有徒手畫線的剪影」，
又指出「脊獸」是建築物的裝飾元素之一。《北京西郊某招待所設計介紹》及《大劇院設計
方案介紹》兩篇文章，分別使用「進深」與「開間」作為建築物的量度單位，這些用字均顯
示出在「社會主義新風格」當中，傳統中國建築元素的重要性。

《建築學報》的介紹性文章亦介紹了政府提倡的集體設計如何被實施。在文章中，個別
建築師的名字不會被提及，但其他人士，特別是非建築專業人士對於建築設計的參與，卻被
視為極具重要性。例如《大劇院設計方案介紹》一文開首即指出在設計過程中，劇院設計組
得到了郵電學院、廣播事業局、新聞電影製片廠的「大力支持協作」，而「通過大搞群眾運
動和集體創作，先後作出40多個比較方案，經過反覆評比，並吸收了其他單位設計方案的優
點，最後確定了目前在平面佈局和建築藝術上一致認為較好的方案」。[68]文中又指建造可以
容納3,000人而不採用電聲的觀眾廳起初被視為不可能的任務，而群眾的敢想敢幹導致「終於
完成了打破陳規的不用電聲的3,000人觀眾廳聲學設計」。儘管在這個設計項目中，群眾其實

68　清華大學建築系劇院設計組1960, P.11

Certain Hotel" and "An Introduction," the modular units of Chinese architecture, "jian" and "jin," are used to describe the dimensions of the building. These terms registered the importance of traditional Chinese elements in the "new" national style of architecture.

Introductory articles in *Architectural Journal* also exemplify how the collective design method encouraged by the government had been implemented. While the names of individual architects were not mentioned, numerous parties, in particular those outside the architectural profession, were noted to have played a vital role in design. For example, at the beginning of "An Introduction," parties such as The State Administration of Radio Film and Television, and the University of Posts and Telecommunication, are identified as having "heavily supported and collaborated with" the design team of the Grand Theater, and it is noted that the collective design method had led to the production of over 40 schemes before a final scheme "agreed by everyone" was selected.[68] The article states that designing an auditorium for 3,000 people without the use of electronic acoustic enhancement systems would have been impossible for architects without the help of the general public — who merely participated in surveys giving their views about the quality of sound in a theater. The article

Perspective, The Grand Theater, Beijing, 1959
大劇院透視圖，北京，1959年

68   Theater Design Group, Tsinghua University 1960, P.11

Perspective of the interior, The Grand Theater, Beijing, 1959
大劇院內部透視圖，北京，1959年

僅參與了音效的現場測定，提供他們對音效的意見，文中卻指「黨和人民群眾才是最懂得建築，最懂得藝術的。」[69]由此可見，在當時《建築學報》的介紹性文章中，大眾在建築設計上的重要性被誇大，而建築師的專業角色則被貶低。

介紹性文章與建築實踐

在毛澤東時期，共產黨宣稱要建立一個平等主義社會，所有建築師都歸屬於同一家設計院，而建築師與群眾在建築設計中被視為同等重要。根據馬克斯主義，建築師是「國家機器上的一顆顆螺絲釘，為社會主義事業建築大廈作貢獻。」[70]整個國家受到嚴格的計劃經濟管制，建築師不能收取任何設計費用，而由於專業人員的工資納入政府工資標準，建築師也只能領取微薄的政府薪酬。當時，設計的個人著作權被全盤否定，而進行個人的建築設計被視為「犯罪」。[71]建築設計透過建築師、工程師、其他專業人士以及使用者的討論產生，而這些

69　清華大學建築系劇院設計組1960, P.15
70　Xue 2006, p.105
71　Xue 2006, p.157

describes the CCP and the general public as those "who understand architecture and art the best."[69] The importance of the general public in design was exaggerated in such articles, while the professional role of architects was minimized.

Introductory Articles and the Practice of Architecture

In the Maoist era, the CCP vowed to create an egalitarian society. Architects working in design institutes belonged to the collective public, and professionals and the general public were considered to have equal importance in architectural design. Under the principles of Marxism, architects were "cogs in a national machine and contributed to the construction of the socialist edifice."[70] They could not charge design fees and were paid meager standard government wages. Individual authorship of design was thoroughly abolished and the pursuit of individualized architectural form was considered a "crime."[71] Designs were developed through discussions among architects, engineers, other professionals, and users. Such designs were frequently changed based on the opinions of different parties. For example, in 1958, urban-based planners and architects were specifically ordered to "go down" to the countryside and work with local peasants to plan commune residential clusters and create design proposals.[72] The introductory articles register the fact that, in the Maoist era, there was no concern for architecture as an autonomous discipline with its own internal knowledge system. The individual status of architects was undermined.[73]

After the establishment of the PRC, economical design was a dominant principle of architecture in China. In 1955, the Soviet Union denounced the tendency toward impractical extravagances in construction and the PRC further reinforced its national austerity policy after that. Nationalistic structures with big roofs and traditional ornamentation were condemned as wasteful and buildings were built according to an ultra-economical standard with the lowest costs possible, as indicated by the abundance of introductory articles on economical designs after the mid-1950s.

69   Theater Design Group, Tsinghua University 1960, P.15
70   Xue 2006, p.105
71   Xue 2006, p.157

72   Lu 2006, p.110
73   Zhu 2009, p.110

設計通常會按照來自不同領域的意見修改。例如於1958年，城市的都市設計者被政府指示下鄉，前往鄉郊與當地農民共同規劃社區住宅群，創作設計提案。[72]正如介紹性文章反映，在毛澤東時期，建築不被視為一個擁有內在教條 (discipline) 的自主學科，建築師的個人地位均不被重視。[73]

在中華人民共和國成立以後，中國鼓吹經濟便宜的設計。1955年，蘇聯指責建築創建普遍存有不切實際、鼓吹奢華的傾向，中華人民共和國於是隨即加強全國性的嚴格節制消費政策。擁有大屋頂及傳統中國建築裝飾的民族形式設計被批評為浪費，而建築物均根據最經濟、成本最低的標準建造。1950年代中期大量介紹經濟設計的介紹性文章可以反映這情況。

介紹性文章向讀者介紹建築論述中的討論話題或對象，而讀者叫自由決定是否參加建築論述。在毛澤東時期，政府透過控制介紹性文章的內容，控制了建築論述中的討論話題或對

72　Lu 2006, p.110
73　Zhu 2009, p.110

Introductory articles introduce topics of discourse on architecture to a wide audience, who may or may not participate in the discourse. In the Maoist era, by controlling the content of introductory articles, the government controlled the subjects of discourse, and the audience only received information that the government wanted them to have. Rather than encouraging a discussion on architecture, the Maoist government used introductory articles illustrating its architectural principles to argue that the principles were beneficial, hoping to create a positive response. The Maoist government required architects to involve the general public in design through discussions and emphasized the importance of "public participation," but the government simultaneously discouraged genuine debate on architecture by heavily manipulating the general public's views. In other words, what the Maoist government promoted was pseudo public participation, and architecture design and construction were in essence controlled by the state.

象，而讀者亦只能接收到政府希望他們得到的訊息。毛澤東政府並不旨在以介紹性文章鼓勵有關建築的討論，卻以有關文章向大眾展示符合政府訂立的建築創建方針的建築物，從而建立方針會帶來益處的論點，希望讀者對方針有正面評價。雖然毛澤東政府要求建築師與公眾進行討論，讓公眾參與設計，並強調「公眾參與」在建築創建中的重要性，但政府卻矛盾地透過操控公眾的意見，妨礙有關建築的自由討論。大眾對於方針的意見被政府操控，換言之，政府鼓勵的是虛假的公眾參與，而建築創建其實由政府大力控制。

COMMENTARIES: THE GOVERNMENT'S ONE-SIDED DEBATE

Commentaries include articles that give opinions — judgments, discriminating points of view, or responses — about issues related to architecture, such as architectural principles, particular buildings, or architectural theories. Commentaries could be written by government news agencies, government officials, reporters, architects, critics, or the general public. They also include interviews in which the interviewees (usually architects or critics) express their opinions. Only commentaries endorsing the views of the government were published in the Maoist era.

Commentaries in Newspapers

During the Maoist era, government news agencies and government officials wrote commentaries to express opinions on different principles for architecture design and construction. The "we" expressing its opinions in the articles was assumed to include the audience, and the opinions expressed by the government were portrayed as the opinions of the public. These commentaries were based on a simple and reductive dichotomy — architectural principles belonged either to "us" or to "them," to the "east" or to the "west," to "socialism" or to "capitalism," to "economical" or to "wasteful." Principles tagged as "we," "the east," "socialist," "economical" belonged to the government side and were promoted, while those labeled "they," "the west," "capitalist," and "wasteful" belonged to the other side and were condemned. For example, in "Against the Wasteful

Practice in Architectural Production," an editorial published in *People's Daily* on 28 March 1955, the government and the general public are referred to as "we," while the pronoun "they" is used to refer to architects who deserve condemnation for their unwillingness to adopt standard designs. In the article, a dormitory for workers built in Qi Qi Ha Er is described as "wasteful" for its relatively high cost, which caused its rent to be two to six times higher than average. Once the dormitory is labeled as "wasteful," it is immediately condemned, with no mention of its functional or aesthetic aspects. Such commentaries established the government's principles for architecture as the standards for "good" designs, which the general public should use to make judgments about buildings.

Commentaries on buildings written by reporters showed that the government was successful in setting the standards for judgment. These commentaries evaluated designs based on the principles for architecture set by the government. In "Problems with the Design of the Capital Theater" written by a reporter and published in *People's Daily* on 23 April 1955, aspects of the building that are "not economical" and "not functional" are identified, described, and condemned. The building is also criticized because it was not designed collectively. In "A Typical 'Western and Weird' Architectural Design," written by a group from the Department of Architecture of Tongji University and published in *Liberation Daily* on 4 May 1974, the design of a hotel is criticized for its resemblance to western architecture, which had been condemned by the Maoist government.

評論：只有政府立場的辯論

　　評論包括表達對建築的判斷、獨特的見解或有關的回應的文章，其內容可能關於建築創建方針、某座建築物或建築理論。建築評論可以由政府新聞機構、政府官員、記者、建築師、評論家又或大眾撰寫，當中也包括建築師或評論家在當中發表意見的訪問稿。在毛澤東時期，只有認同政府意見的評論才會出版。

報章評論

　　在毛澤東時期，政府新聞機構及政府官員均會撰寫評論，表達他們對建築創建方針的意見。文章中，政府慣常使用第一人稱「我們」表達其意見，而讀者均被視為「我們」的一份子，故政府的意見往往被描繪成讀者的意見。這些意見反映出簡單及片面的二分法，被評論的建築創建方針要麼歸屬於「我們」，要麼歸屬於「他們」；要麼歸屬於「東方」，要麼歸屬於「西方」；要麼歸屬於「社會主義」，要麼歸屬於「資本主義」；要麼歸屬於「經濟」，要麼歸屬於「浪費」。「我們」、「東方」、「社會主義」、「經濟」等都代表認同政府的意見，備受推廣；「他們」、「西方」、「資本主義」、「浪費」等都代表不認同政府的意見，備受批評。例如在1955年3月28日《人民日報》出版的《反對建築中的浪費現象》一

Capital Theater, Beijing, 1955
首都劇場，北京，1955年

The general public, through letters to the newspapers, could engage in a debate with reporters on whether designs written about in commentaries were evaluated "correctly," but such debates were invariably based on a literal interpretation of the government's principles. The aim of the debate was simply to identify designs that exemplified the principles. The debate did not question the underlying assumptions on which the architectural principles were based. The government had successfully established the framework for evaluation of building designs, and manipulated the scope of opinions that appeared in the commentaries in newspapers.

Commentaries in *Architectural Journal*

As noted earlier, introductory articles in *Architectural Journal* also invited comments, and commentaries registered debates on designs introduced in the original articles. There were also commentaries discussing the meanings of terms used in the principles for architecture design and construction,[74] analyzing the terms and expressing opinions not based on literal interpretation and

74 Commentaries discussing the meanings of the terms used in the principles for architecture design and construction could also be regarded as government propaganda writings because the aim of such articles was to promote the principles. The characteristics of these commentaries about the terms used in the principles have been discussed in the section "Government Propaganda Writings in *Architectural Journal*" through examples of writings centered around "A Discussion on Architecture as Art in Relation to Aesthetics and National Form" published in 1955.

一个"又洋又怪"的建筑设计典型

批判教学领域里的崇洋复古思想

"A Typical 'Western and Weird' Architectural Design," *Liberation Daily*, 4 May 1957
《一個『又洋又怪』的建築設計典型》，《解放日報》，1957年5月4日文，政府及大眾同時均以第一人稱「我們」表示，而拒絕採用標準設計、備受批評的建築師則以第三人稱「他們」稱呼。文中提及一所在齊齊哈爾建設的員工宿舍，因為其相對較高的建築成本，導致租金比平均價格高出二至六倍，員工宿舍因此被形容為「浪費」；被視作「浪費」的員工宿舍隨即受到批評，而宿舍的功能性及其美學層面當中的可取之處均完全未被提及。在這些有關政府訂立的建築創建方針的評論中，方針被塑造成「理想」設計的標準，而大眾可根據這些標準對不同建築物作出評價。

在毛澤東時期由記者撰寫的建築評論，顯示當時的政府成功確立了對建築判斷的標準。在這些評論中，對建築設計的評價均以政府訂立的建築創建方針為基礎。例如在1955年4月23日於《人民日報》出版、由記者馬浩然撰寫的《首都劇場設計中存在的問題》中，劇場「不經濟」、「不實用」的層面均被逐點指出，然後詳細描述及作出批評，而劇場亦被批評為沒有採納集體設計。在1974年5月4日於《解放日報》出版、由同濟大學「五‧七」公社建築學專業黨支部撰寫的《一個『又洋又怪』的建築設計典型》一文，當中討論的酒店設計因為近似西方建築而備受批評，而西方建築當時正遭毛澤東政府唾棄。

雖然大眾可以透過去信報館，與評論的作者辯論一項建築設計是否根據政府的建築創建方

simple dichotomy. Participants in such debates included "renowned architectural experts, practitioners of design institutes, teachers and students from architecture schools, newspaper journalists, and average citizens."[75] Like newspaper reporters, the authors of the commentaries in *Architectural Journal*, mostly architectural professionals, based their evaluations of building designs on the principles for architecture set by the government, though expressed in more technical and architectural terms and often suggesting "improved" design schemes.

The introductory article "Qianmen Hotel,"[76] written by architect Zhang Bo and published in *Architectural Journal* in 1957, initiated a debate about the design of the building. Zhou Buyi from Tsinghua University and architects Ye Zugui and Ye Yaofu, respectively, published "A Discussion on the Architectural Design of our Country through the Analysis of Several New Buildings in Beijing"[77] and "Comments on the Design of Qianmen Hotel and a Discussion with Mr. Zhang Bo"[78] in the same year, criticizing Zhang's design because it sacrificed the functional and economical aspects for the sake of

aesthetics. In these commentaries, the floor plans, structure of the building, and construction costs are all evaluated based on the principle "functional, economical, and delightful if conditions permit." For example, Zhou criticizes the building for having 14 fake columns for aesthetic reasons, and Ye Zugui and Ye Yaofu criticize Zhang for unnecessarily increasing the area of the bathrooms for the sake of the proportion of the façade. Zhang in turn published "Comments on Commentaries on Qianmen Hotel and a Further Explanation of the Design,"[79] defending his design, again based on the "functional, economical, and delightful if conditions permit" principle. In other words, judgments on designs made by architectural professionals were also based on interpretations of the principles for architecture set by the government.

Architectural Journal also viewed opinions of the general public as important and published letters from average citizens as well as reprinting articles originally published in newspapers. For example, "The Extravagant Yet Impractical Hotel in the Western Suburbs," an article by reporter Fan Rongkang

75   Cheng 2005, p.49
76   *Architectural Journal*, 1957(01), p.27-38
77   *Architectural Journal*, 1957(03), p.41-50
78   *Architectural Journal*, 1957(04), p.46-52

79   *Architectural Journal*, 1957(06), p.47-55

針被「正確」評估，但在這些辯論當中，方針均只跟從字面意義被解讀。這些辯論旨在找出真正彰顯方針的建築物，而非旨在挑戰建築創建的基礎原則。政府成功地建立了評價建築物的標準，並控制了出現在報章的評論的範疇。

《建築學報》的評論

如本書較早前部分所述，《建築學報》的介紹性文章邀請讀者就所介紹的建築表達意見，而《建築學報》的評論文章反映讀者確有參與有關建築的辯論。另外，《建築學報》亦有刊登辯論建築創建方針所採用的字眼的含義的文章，[74]反映了《建築學報》的作者對有關字眼會進行分析，而並非基於對字面意義的基本解讀以及簡單的二分法發表意見。這些辯論的參與者包括「有解放前即已成名的建築專家，有各個設計院的普通建築工作者，有建築院校的青年師生，也有綜合報社的記者和普通的市民」。[75]與報章記者一樣，《建築學報》的作者（主要為建築專業人士）以政府訂立的建築創建方針作為評價建築設計的基礎，但這些討論均有一個更為技術性及建築上的層面，而《建築學報》的作者亦會提出「改善」建築設計的方案。

於1957年《建築學報》出版、由建築師張鎛撰寫的《前門飯店》[76]一文，開展了一場有關該設計的辯論。清華大學的周卜頤同年撰寫了《從北京幾座新建築的分析談我國的建築創作》，[77]而葉祖貴（城建部北京民用建築設計院建築師）、葉耀富（鐵道部科學研究院建築師）亦於同年發表了《對前門飯店設計的幾點意見與張鎛先生商榷》[78]一文，批評張鎛的設計為求美觀，犧牲了實用及經濟的原則。在這些評論文章中，前門飯店的平面圖、結構、建築成本等都根據「實用、經濟、在可能條件下注意美觀」的原則被討論。例如周卜頤批評張鎛「為了追求藝術構圖，在已經很密的十四根鋼筋混凝土柱子的大廳中，又添加了十四根假柱……很顯然，建築創作在這裡還沒有從磚石結構所產生的比例中解放出來，還在不斷追求這種古老

74　這些辯論建築創建方針所採用字眼含義的文章亦可被視為政府宣傳性文章，因為有關文章旨在宣揚方針。這些文章的特點已在「《建築學報》的政府宣傳性文章」一部分討論，該部分分析了環繞1955年出版的《論建築藝術與美及民族形式》的一系列文章。

75　程曉喜 2005, p.4
76　《建築學報》，1957(01), p.27-38
77　《建築學報》，1957(03), p.41-50
78　《建築學報》，1957(04), p.46-52

criticizing the hotel that was originally published in *People's Daily* on 28 April 1955, was also published in the first issue of *Architectural Journal* that year. "People Ask Architects to Criticize and Self-Criticize,"[80] a letter to the editor of *People's Daily* criticizing the former Guangzhou Culture Park, was published in 1954 together with a response from *Architectural Journal* saying that average citizens had the "right" to require architects to self-criticize. The journal also asks the architect of the former Guangzhou Culture Park to pay attention to the letter. *Architectural Journal* served as the platform for discourse on architecture among both architectural professionals and the general public in the Maoist era.

CLOCKWISE 順時針:
Exterior view, Qianmen Hotel, Beijing, 1956
前門飯店外部景觀，北京，1956年

Interior view of a room, Qianmen Hotel, Beijing, 1956
前門飯店房間室內景觀，北京，1956年

Interior view, Qianmen Hotel, Beijing, 1956
前門飯店室內景觀，北京，1956年

80 *Architectural Journal*, 1954(02) p.122-124

比例的藝術構圖。」葉祖貴及葉耀富批評張鎛為了追求「立面向前突出一大片」，將衛生間的面積增大，卻並未增大衛生間的活動面積。張鎛於是出版《對前門飯店設計評論的意見和補充説明》，[79]根據「實用、經濟、在可能條件下注意美觀」的原則為自己的設計辯護。換言之，建築專業人士也是根據政府訂立的建築創建方針來判斷設計。

另外，《建築學報》非常重視大眾的意見，會發表讀者來信或轉載曾於報章刊載的讀者來函。例如1955年第一期的《建築學報》刊登了由記者范榮康撰寫、於1955年4月28日在《人民日報》發表的《華而不實的西郊招待所》，該篇文章批評了招待所的設計。1954年，《建築學報》刊登了《人民日報》的讀者來信，題為《人們要求建築師展開批評和自我批評》，[80]該讀者就廣州的嶺南文物宮設計作出批評；《建築學報》於同版刊登回應，指出「人民有權利要求我們（建築師）展開批評和自我批評」，又指「希望廣州文物宮的設計建築師予以重視」。由此可見，《建築學報》在毛澤東時期，是建築專業人士及大眾之間的建築論述的平台。

79《建築學報》，1957(06), p.47-55
80《建築學報》，1954(02), p.122-124

After 1978

一
九
七
八
年
以
後

INTRODUCTORY ARTICLES: RE-EMERGENCE OF THE INDIVIDUAL ARCHITECT

Introductory Articles in the Mass Media

Introductory articles with a greater variety of themes began to appear in newspapers and magazines as China opened up in 1978. Articles introducing particular buildings continued to appear in the mass media in the post-Mao era, and began to include buildings designed by architects from western capitalist countries, which had never been written about in the Maoist era. Interviews in which individual architects explain their own works, as well as profile stories on both Chinese and western architects, began to appear. Introductory articles also became available on the internet in the late 1990s. In the 1990s, as Claudio Greco, an engineer and architect practicing in Rome and Beijing, puts it in *Beijing: The New City*, "the doors to direct, low-cost knowledge had opened to Chinese youngsters, adolescents, students, and professionals."[81]

Almost immediately after the end of the Cultural Revolution, individual architects began to be identified. Although there were not many noticeable profile stories on architects before the late 1990s, articles introducing specific buildings had parts dedicated to introducing their architects. On 29 September 1979, *Wenhui Bao* published "The Song of an Expert in Traditional Chinese Architecture — an Interview with Tongji University Professor Chen Congzhou" ("The Song"), describing Chen's installation of a Suzhou garden in the Metropolitan Museum of Art in New York. "I.M. Pei's 'New Chapter of Music'" ("I.M. Pei"), introducing the Fragrant Hill Hotel, was published in *People's Daily* on 8 November 1982. In these two articles, more than half the content is devoted to introducing the architects, often using anecdotes to portray them as individual characters. "The Song" includes anecdotes about Chen's extensive research on traditional Chinese gardens. The article describes in detail how Chen "risked his life" as he entered the dilapidated Tiger Hill Pagoda in Suzhou, portraying him as a hero. An anecdote in "I.M. Pei" describes how Pei removed 30 houses from his original design for the Fragrant Hill Hotel to protect the trees in Fragrant Hill, and Pei is depicted as an architect who treats his designs very seriously. These anecdotes give a human dimension to the introductory articles. Architects themselves, not just their architectural artefacts, had become subjects worth writing about.

Introductory articles in the post-Mao era also emphasized the importance of research and

81   Greco 2008, p.92

介紹性文章：建築師重新嶄露頭角

大眾傳媒的介紹性文章

1978年，中國實行改革開放政策，不同類型的介紹性文章開始出現。在毛澤東時期結束後，大眾媒體繼續刊登介紹特定建築物的文章，而所介紹的建築物包括在毛澤東時期從未被提及、由西方資本主義國家建築師設計的作品。這個時期的介紹性文章亦包括建築師談及其作品的訪談，以及中國和西方建築師的人物特寫。1990年代後期，介紹性文章亦開始在互聯網出現，如於羅馬及北京執業的工程師兼建築師克勞迪奧‧格萊克 (Claudio Greco) 在《北京‧嶄新的城市》(Beijing: The New City) 一書所述，90年代開始，「中國的年青人、青少年、學生及專業人士開始能直接、低成本地接觸到知識。」[81]

文化大革命結束後，個別建築師的獨立地位幾乎被立刻肯定。在1990年代後期以前，大眾傳媒並沒有太多建築師的人物特寫，但一些介紹建築物的文章往往會向讀者提及並介紹建築師。1979年9月29日《文匯報》刊登的《古建築家之歌 ─ 訪同濟大學教授陳從周》一文，介紹陳從周在紐約大都會藝術博物館的蘇州園林裝置，而1982年11月8日於《人民日報》刊登

的《貝聿銘的『新樂章』》一文，則介紹香山飯店；兩篇文章超過一半內容均用作介紹建築師，記載建築師的設計軼事，為建築師塑造獨立角色。《古建築家之歌 ─ 訪同濟大學教授陳從周》一文，記述了陳從周研究中國傳統園林的故事，文中詳細描述陳從周「冒著生命危險」，爬上蘇州虎丘的古塔進行考察，將他塑造成英雄；《貝聿銘的『新樂章』》一文提到貝聿銘「為了盡可能保護香山的古樹，他幾易設計圖紙，並為此砍掉了30間房子」，並將貝聿銘形容為極度認真對待設計的建築師。上述有關建築師的軼事為介紹性文章帶來人性化的層面，可見文革結束以後，除了建築物以外，建築師本身也是值得書寫的題材。

毛澤東時期結束以後在大眾傳媒出現的介紹性文章，反映了研究知識對於建築的重要性。在《古建築家之歌 ─ 訪同濟大學教授陳從周》一文，陳從周被形容為新中國的建設事業依賴的知識分子，「對中國各地園林可謂瞭如指掌」，而且擁有「堅強毅力和刻苦認真做學問的精神」。陳從周發現了蘇州最古老的園林喬園，被形容成「為祖國找出了巨大的珍寶」。

---

81 Greco 2008, p.92

knowledge. "The Song" describes Chen as one of the intellectuals that China needs, because of his "thorough knowledge of the gardens in different parts of China" and his "hard work and perseverance in research works." His discovery of Qiaoyuan, one of the oldest gardens in Suzhou, is referred to as "a great treasure of the country." In "I.M. Pei," the author describes how Pei values research. In the years when the design and construction of Fragrant Hill Hotel was proceeding, Pei, based in the US, "traveled many times to Suzhou, Yangzhou, and Hangzhou to study the gardens," and his design is said to reflect this thorough research. As the Maoist era ended, architecture writings began to recognize the importance of the relationship between research and knowledge on the one hand, and architectural design and construction on the other. The professional status of architects gained increasing respect, and their individual creativity was emphasized.

Themes of introductory articles in newspapers underwent another significant change around the millennium, with a proliferation of articles about iconic architecture in both China and foreign countries. In almost all cases, the buildings are affirmatively labeled as "icons" or "landmarks," and the articles describe in detail the form, façade, and construction materials to illustrate both the individual creativity of the architects and the iconic status of the buildings. The basic function of buildings is noted, but the articles seldom describe how functional needs have been taken into

"The Song of an Expert in Traditional Chinese Architecture - an Interview with Tongji University Professor Chen Congzhou," *Wenhui Bao*, 29 September 1979
《古建築家之歌 — 訪同濟大學教授陳從周》，《文匯報》，1979年9月29日

在《貝聿銘的『新樂章』》一文，作者形容了貝聿銘對研究工作的重視：在香山飯店設計及建造期間，在美國定居的貝聿銘從勘察香山飯店的地形到建成的幾年中，「風塵僕僕地往來於紐約、北京之間，多次到蘇州、揚州、杭州參觀考察園林，拍了不少民居和多種窗戶式樣的照片」，而有關資料「在香山飯店建設中體現得很充分」。毛澤東時期結束後，建築寫作肯定研究知識與建築之間的關係，建築師的專業地位重新得到尊重，其個人創造力也備受肯定。

於報章刊登的介紹性文章的主題於大概2000年間經歷了另一次重大改變，其時，大量介紹建於中國及世界各地地標式建築的文章相繼出現。幾乎所有這類文章都將所介紹的地標式建築標籤為「標誌」或「地標」，而這些詞彙在有關文章中均帶有正面意義；文章小詳細介紹建築的外貌、形式、立面及建築材料等，以展示建築師的個人創意及建築物的地標性。這類文章會提及建築物的基本功能，但很少詳細談到設計如何考慮到建築物的功能性。文章提及興建建築物的龐大成本，旨在表示中國擁有足夠的國力及財富去建造地標式建築。例如在2007年9月18日《人民日報》出版的《解讀國家大劇院》中，記者將保羅‧安德魯(Paul

consideration in the design process. The huge costs of the buildings are mentioned not as mere facts, but to emphasize that China has the wealth and power to pay for the construction of iconic architecture. In "An Interpretation of National Grand Theater" published in *People's Daily* on 18 September 2007, the reporter describes the building by Paul Andreu as a landmark that attracts attention, and quotes a Beijing government official saying that the Theater is "the biggest iconic cultural facility that the government has ever invested in," "an icon showing the level of civilization of the city [Beijing]," and "a symbol of the overall power of the country." In a way clearly designed to impress readers, the article uses terms like "the most" and "the first" to describe the look of the Theater, and uses huge numbers to describe the scale of the project. For example, the massive amount of materials required to cover the shell structure of the Theater — over 20,000 titanium plates and over 1,200 pieces of glass — is emphasized. The National Grand Theater is said to have solved "a world class construction problem," with "the biggest dome in China," boasting "a perimeter of over 6,000 meters." The introductory articles seem to treat the building as an icon that manifests the country's image as a key international player, rather than as an architectural artefact per se.

The emphasis on iconic architecture in China's mass media is also evident in the abundance of profile stories about western star architects who have designed iconic architecture, whether in China

National Grand Theater, Beijing, 2007, Photography by Sylvia Chan
國家大劇院，北京，2007年，陳曼霞攝

Andreu) 設計的國家大劇院形容為「長安街上一座吸引眼球的新地標」，並引述北京市有關負責人稱，「國家大劇院是中國政府面向21世紀投資興建的最大的標誌性文化設施，是改革開放以來國家綜合實力不斷增強的充分展示」，而「它的建成及投入使用是城市文明層次的標誌、國家綜合實力的體現和當代傑出文化的象徵。」文章然後詳細介紹大劇院的造型，經常運用「最大」、「第一」等詞彙，並引用龐大數據表示建築物的規模，務求令讀者留下深刻印象。例如文中強調「國家大劇院的殼體表面由2萬多塊鈦金屬板和1,200多塊超白透明玻璃組成」、「高46.285米，東西軸跨度212米、南北軸跨度144米，周長達6,000多米」，是「中國第一大穹頂」，而其建成更被形容為解決了「一個世界級的施工難題」。這類文章似乎意在表明國家大劇院是一個地標，足以宣示國家作為國際事務重大參與者的形象，卻非旨在於建築論述的層面討論建築物本身，介紹其對於建築創建的影響。

　　大量曾於中國或世界各地設計地標式建築的西方明星級建築師的人物特寫，亦可反映中國傳媒對地標式建築的重視。此類人物特寫傾向神化建築師，將他們形容為擁有驚人才華的天才。在2006年7月17日於《新民晚報》出版、題為《來自巴格達的傳奇女建築師扎哈》的扎

Jean Nouvel, courtesy of Gaston Bergeret
讓‧努維爾，Gaston Bergeret 提供

or elsewhere. These profiles tend to apotheosize the architects, often describing them as geniuses with talents beyond the imagination of ordinary people. A profile on Zaha Hadid titled "The Legendary Female Architect from Baghdad, Zaha" and published in *Xinmin Evening News* on 17 July 2006, describes Hadid as a "legendary" figure, who can "manipulate the space just by following her heart." It goes on to say that ordinary people "could never imagine the way she deals with space." Hadid has built projects in China, including Guangzhou Opera House, opened in 2010, and Galaxy Soho in Beijing (still under construction at the time of writing). On 24 April 2010, a profile story on Jean Nouvel[82] titled "Father of 'Rose of the Desert': a Delirious Dreamer" was published in *Guangzhou Daily*. "Rose of the Desert" refers to the National Museum of Qatar, which Nouvel designed. In the article, Nouvel is referred to as "the most famous contemporary architect in France" and "a genius with fathomless talents," who is fighting against architecture that is banal and soulless. Both articles try to establish a strong image for the architects — Hadid as a "harsh" architect always wearing brand-name high-heels and Nouvel as a "hedonist" always dressed in black. These details establish the architects themselves as icons, alongside their iconic designs. Star architects' names are used like brand names and their

National Museum of Qatar, Doha, designed in 2010, courtesy of Ateliers Jean Nouvel
卡塔爾國家博物館新館，多哈，2010年設計，Ateliers Jean Nouvel 提供

82   Jean Nouvel has no built project in China.

Zaha Hadid, courtesy of Marco Grob
扎哈・哈迪，Marco Grob 提供

Galaxy Soho, Beijing, designed in 2009, courtesy of Zaha Hadid Architects
銀河SOHO，北京，2009年設計，Zaha Hadid Architects 提供

works become branded commodities, with the introductory articles showing the audience models of allegedly good taste.[83]

Chinese architects and their works receive less attention from the print media in comparison. There are relatively sporadic articles on them, and these often compare their buildings to the iconic works of western architects, emphasizing the Chinese essence of the former as well as the Chinese architects' understanding of their own culture. "Traditional Chinese Music Staged in Modern Architecture" ("Traditional Chinese Music") published in *Yangcheng Evening News* on 27 August 2009, introduces the Guangdong Xinghai Performance Group Office Building in Ersha, designed by Chinese architect Li Shaoyun, and gives a detailed description of Chinese elements in the building's design. The article describes Li's belief that while the architecture of the new century should be avant-garde, "avant-garde architecture" should not be built at huge expense, as in the cases of Guangzhou Opera House, CCTV Headquarters, and National Grand Theater. Instead, the article emphasizes that Chinese "essence" is more important than iconicity, and upholds designs that are "both international and local" and show "a deep understanding of both modern architecture and the Chinese concept

83   Markus 2002, p.110

"Traditional Chinese Music Staged in Modern Architecture," *Yangcheng Evening News*, 27 August 2009
《現代建築上演絲竹雅韻》，
《羊城晚報》，2009年8月27日

哈・哈迪 (Zaha Hadid) 人物特寫中，哈迪被形容為「傳奇」人物，「操縱空間隨心所欲，就像揉麵團或是切菜一樣」，而一般人「永遠想像不出她處理空間的方式」。哈迪在中國有不同項目，包括2010年開幕的廣州大劇院及在北京興建中的銀河SOHO。在2010年4月24日於《廣州日報》出版、題為《『沙漠玫瑰』之父：瘋狂幻想家》的讓・努維爾 (Jean Nouvel) [82]人物特寫，設計卡塔爾國家博物館新館的努維爾被稱為「法國當代最著名建築師」及「一個深不可測的天才」，「拋出一個又一個石破天驚的設計，和那些平庸、缺少靈魂的建築抗爭到底」。此外，兩篇文章都試圖建立兩名建築師的獨特形象 ── 哈迪是「個性苛刻」的建築師，「一身標誌性的打扮常常是：束腰上衣，修身長褲，名牌鞋，從頭到腳一身黑」，而努維爾則是總是一襲黑衣的「享樂主義者」。這些細緻描述將建築師本身塑造成標誌，與他們的地標式建築並行。設計師的名字猶如品牌般被利用，他們的作品是品牌產品，而明星建築師的人物特寫及其作品的介紹性文章均意在向讀者介紹一種所謂公認的優良品味。[83]

相對地，中國建築師及其作品並未受到相同重視，有關他們的文章相對較少，而這些文章通常將所介紹的建築物，即由中國建築師設計的建築物，與由西方建築師建造的地標式建築比較，強調前者的中國特色，以及中國建築師對其本身文化的理解。2009年8月27日於《羊城晚報》刊登的《現代建築上演絲竹雅韻》，介紹了由廣州市城市規劃勘測設計研究院副總規劃師、城市與建築設計所所長、原天作設計公司設計總監李少雲設計、位於二沙島的廣東星海演藝集團辦公樓，並詳細描述了建築物展示的「中國的氣質和神韻」。文中提到李少雲的意見，指「新世紀的建築應該是前衛的，但這種前衛不可能像扎哈的廣州歌劇院，或是像北京的央視大樓和國家大劇院那樣以昂貴的代價來獲得」。文中強調中國「元素」相對於地標性的重要性，鼓勵「既是國際的，又是本土的」建築，展示「設計師對現代建築設計和中國式審美意境的深刻認知」。在文中，中國文化被形容為「深遠」，而文中強調較抽象難懂的「氣質」，而非中國傳統建築結構元素。《現代建築上演絲竹雅韻》這類訪問中國建

82　讓・努維爾在中國並無建設項目。
83　Markus 2002, p.110

of aesthetics." The article describes the "profound" nature of Chinese culture, and the abstract and difficult-to-understand nature of Chinese "temperament," rather than emphasizing the formal elements of traditional Chinese architecture. Articles like "Traditional Chinese Music," where Chinese architects are interviewed, often emphasize the uniqueness of Chinese culture, as if suggesting that Chinese architects are irreplaceable by western star architects. Similar articles are more widely available on the internet, in particular at the "Conversation with the Architecture Profession" section of abbs.com.cn, one of the most widely visited architecture websites in China.

Introductory Articles in Field Journals

Architectural Journal has published an increasing variety of content since the end of the Cultural Revolution, and new journals including *Huazhong Architecture*, *New Architecture*, *Time + Architecture* and *World Architecture* were launched in the 1980s. Introductory articles in these journals focus on different themes, introducing works and architectural practices in both China and other countries.

Articles introducing the works of Chinese architects have continued to appear in field journals in the post-Mao era. Until the late 1990s, such introductory articles resembled those in the Maoist era, giving detailed descriptions of the buildings, from overall organization to construction details, focusing

Guo'an Theater, Beijing, 1994
國安劇院，北京，1994年

築師的文章，通常強調中國文化的獨特性，企圖暗示中國建築師始終不能被西方建築明星取代。類似的文章目前於互聯網上比較流行，全國最流行的建築網站之 ── abbs.com.cn「對話建築界」一欄目經常發表國內外建築師的人物特寫故事。

專業期刊的介紹性文章

在文革結束以後，《建築學報》的內容不斷豐富，而《華中建築》、《新建築》、《時代建築》、《世界建築》等專業期刊於1980年代起陸續出現。這些專業期刊的介紹性文章有不同主題，介紹中國及其他國家的建築作品及建築師事務所。

毛澤東時期結束以後，介紹中國建築師作品的文章繼續在專業期刊出現。至1990年代末段，此類介紹性文章與毛澤東時期的介紹性文章分別不大，兩個時期的文章均詳細描寫建築物的整體佈局以至建築細部，並以建築物的功能性為焦點。例如於1996年《建築學報》出版的《國安劇院 ── 一座適用、經濟、新穎、大方的劇場》[84]一文，與1960年《建築學報》出版

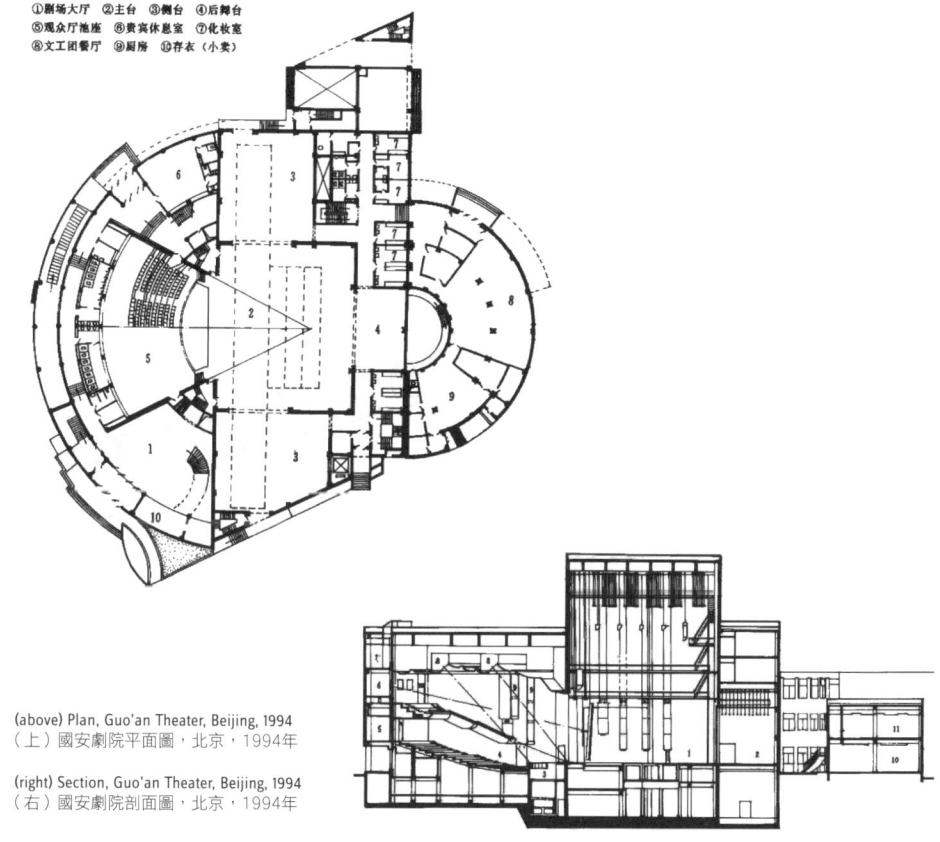

(above) Plan, Guo'an Theater, Beijing, 1994
（上）國安劇院平面圖，北京，1994年

(right) Section, Guo'an Theater, Beijing, 1994
（右）國安劇院剖面圖，北京，1994年

84 《建築學報》，1996(05)，p.39-42

on function. In terms of writing style, for example, "Guo'an Theater — a Theater that is Functional, Economical, Novel, Elegant,"[84] published in *Architectural Journal* in 1996, closely resembles "An Introduction of the Design Scheme for the Grand Theater"[85] published in 1960, except that terms exaggerating the importance of the general public are omitted in the former. These articles continue to provide technical information and serve as references for architects.

While architecture from western capitalist countries was condemned in the Maoist era, introductory articles on buildings or practices in western capitalist countries began to appear in field journals in the late 1970s. Since the 1980s, articles even began to portray them as role models for China's modern architectural development. The first noticeable introductory article on architecture from western capitalist countries was "Architectural Designs of Foreign Exhibition Halls and Museums,"[86] published in *Architectural Journal* in 1979. However, the article does not focus on a particular museum or exhibition hall outside China, but attempts to give general guidelines for designing museums and exhibition halls based on the buildings introduced. The article first states a

guideline, then introduces buildings that illustrate the guideline. The Solomon R. Guggenheim Museum and Centre Pompidou, for instance, are used to illustrate the use of central voids and flexible spatial organization in museums. The audience is not given a full picture of the overall building, but only particular aspects that the author chooses to highlight.

With the start of *World Architecture* in 1980, introductory articles on specific buildings in the west became available to readers. Unlike articles on buildings designed by local architects, articles introducing the latest designs in the west, until recently, were often much briefer, offering only overviews without technical construction information. Detailed articles were relatively sporadic. In the 1980s, buildings designed by western architectural firms — and the firms themselves — were often highly acclaimed in introductory articles. In "SOM's Works and its Method of Work"[87] published in *World Architecture* in 1981, the authors describe the company in a tone of amazement and admiration, as a company "with a great reputation both in the US and outside," "deeply trusted by its clients," and "having the most appropriate number of professionals." The article also describes the typical

84   *Architectural Journal*, 1996(05), p.39-42
85   This article has been discussed in the section "Introductory Articles in *Architectural Journal* in the Maoist era."
86   *Architectural Journal*, 1979(02), p.38-41

87   *World Architecture*, 1981(06), p.56-57

的《大劇院設計方案介紹》[85]寫法非常相似，儘管前者並未強調公眾參與建築創建的重要性。此類文章繼續提供技術資訊，供建築師參考。

在毛澤東時期，西方資本主義國家的建築備受唾棄，但自1970年代末起，介紹西方資本主義國家建築及建築師事務所的介紹性文章相繼出現；自1980年代起，西方資本主義國家的建築更被視為中國當代建築發展的榜樣。《建築學報》首篇明確介紹西方資本主義國家建築的文章是1979年出版的《國外展覽館、博物館的建築設計》。[86]不過，文章的焦點不是中國境外個別的展覽館或博物館，卻旨在從所介紹的建築物歸納出設計展覽館或博物館的指引。文中首先提出設計指引，然後簡略描述應用了有關指引的建築物。例如文中分別以古根漢博物館及龐比度中心為例，闡釋建築物運用中庭空間的概念以及博物館的靈活空間佈置。讀者不能從文中了解到被介紹的建築物的整體面貌，只能認識作者選擇介紹的個別部分。

隨著《世界建築》於1980年面世，讀者開始接觸到介紹西方個別建築物的介紹性文章。與介紹本地建築師作品的介紹性文章不同，介紹西方最新設計的文章通常甚為簡短，只提供建築物概要，並無有關建造的技術資訊。但近期開始，較詳細地介紹西方建築物的文章更廣泛出版。在1980年代，這些介紹性文章都高度表揚西方建築師事務所及其作品。例如在1981年《世界建築》出版的《SOM事務所的作品及其工作方法》，[87]作者以讚嘆及仰慕的論調撰寫文章，指 SOM「是美國最大的建築事務所之一，在美國及國外享有盛譽」、「深得業主門的信任」及「有最全的專業」。文中亦介紹了 SOM 的日常管理策略，例如公司如何聘請人手以及如何進行討論與設計，指出「他們是屬於資本主義的，但他們建築創作中的一些經驗和工作方法，仍有可取之處」，換言之，中國的建築師事務所應向這些國際事務所學習。

於人約2000年，專業期刊陸續刊登有關國外建築師設計的地標式建築的文章，而有關國外建築師事務所的專題集亦零星出現，例如《世界建築》於2003(02)號出版了OMA的專題集。這些文章通常由建築專業人士撰寫，其寫作方式與於大眾傳媒刊登的介紹性文章相似，往往表達

85　本書已在毛澤東時期《建築學報》的介紹性文章部分討論此文章。
86　《建築學報》，1979(02), p.38-41

87　《世界建築》，1981(06), p.56-57

Rocco Yim, courtesy of Rocco Design Architects
嚴迅奇，許李嚴建築師事務有限公司提供

management strategy of SOM, ranging from its hiring practices to how the firm carries out discussions and makes design decisions. It clearly suggests that architects in China should learn from the practices of such international companies.

As introductory articles on iconic architecture by foreign architects began to appear in field journals, monographs on foreign architectural practices also started to appear sporadically. For example, OMA's monograph was published in *World Architecture* in 2003(02). These articles, often written by architecture professionals, employ a tone similar to those in the mass media to describe the iconic buildings, conveying a sense of awe. For example, in "A Dream Realized, on National Grand Theater"[88] ("A Dream Realized"), written by Zhou Qinglin from the project management department of the National Grand Theater and published in *Architectural Journal* in 2008, the Theater is described as showing "the technological standard and overall power of the country," and the interior space of the Theater is described as "unique in the world." However, while articles in field journals do register the iconic status of buildings, terms such as "icon" or "landmark" are seldom used. The articles also emphasize the functions of iconic buildings and their connections with the environment. "A Dream

88   *Architectural Journal*, 2008(01), p.59-61

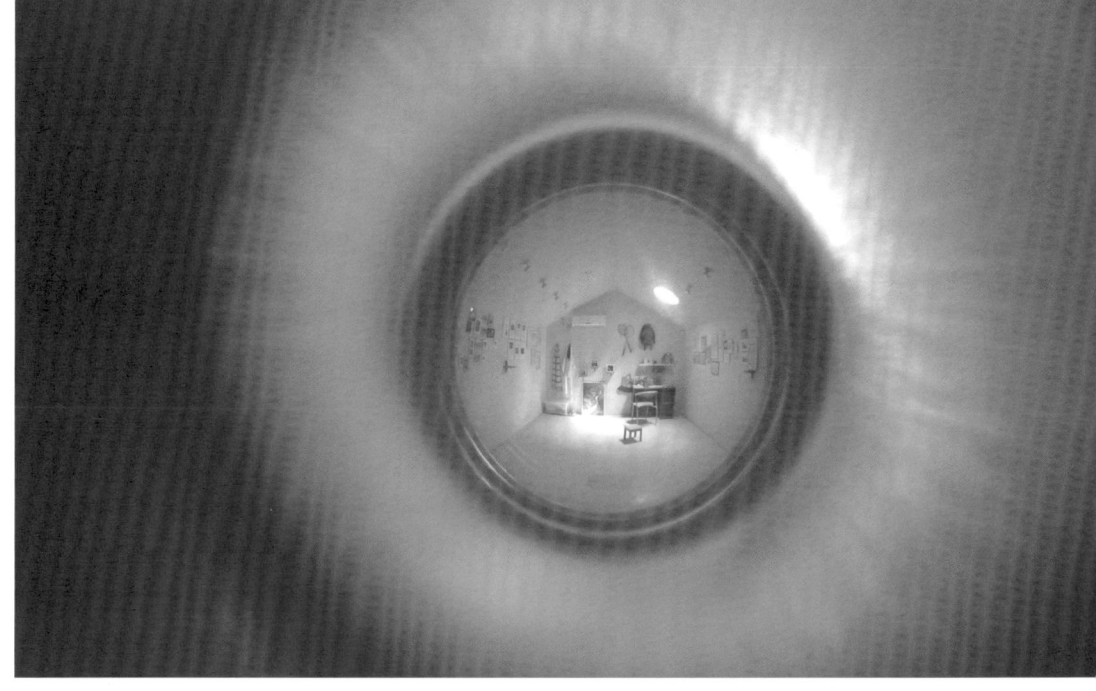

Hu Huishan Memorial House, Sichuan, 2009, courtesy of Jiakun Architects
胡慧姍紀念館，四川，2009年，
家琨建築設計事務所提供

出對於地標式建築的讚嘆。例如在2008年《建築學報》出版、由國家大劇院工程業主委員會的
周慶琳撰寫的《夢想實現 — 記國家大劇院》[88]一文，大劇院被形容為「走過了多少艱困曲折的
道路，經歷了多少耐人尋味的故事，終於在一種樂觀的氣氛中擺在世人面前」，並擁有
「舉世無雙的室內空間」。不過，儘管專業期刊肯定此類建築物的地標性，其介紹性文章甚少
直接使用「地標」或「標誌」等字眼，反而強調地標式建築的功能及它們與環境的關係。在
《夢想實現 — 記國家大劇院》一文，劇院每個劇場的功能都被詳細描述。周慶琳亦指出，
「當你踏下公共汽車的踏板來到大劇院前廣場時，呈現在你面前的是一片向內彎曲的弧型牆
面，歡迎你的到來」、在決定擴展工程用地時，「第一次擴下來使得主體建築很難同周邊的
建築找上關係，再決定向南擴展，使主體建築的東西軸線同人民大會堂的東西軸線相吻合」、
「而簡潔無華的紅色牆體與天安門城牆遙相呼應」等。專業期刊的文章將標誌性建築視為設計
出眾的建築，而非單純的地標。

　　與大眾傳媒不同，專業期刊並未被介紹地標式建築的文章壟斷，反而以較平衡的比重介紹
國外建築師的地標式建築與本地建築師的作品。專業期刊與大眾傳媒在介紹本地建築師的作

Liu Jiakun, courtesy of Jiakun Architects
劉家琨，家琨建築設計事務所提供

Beijing Digital Press Information Center, Beijing, 2008,
courtesy of China Architecture Design & Research Group
北京數字出版信息中心，北京，2008年，
中國建築設計研究院提供

Realized" describes in detail the function of each hall in the Theater. Zhou also notes that the design of

the Theater has taken the surroundings into serious consideration. For instance, the axis of the Theater

is a continuation of the axis of the Great Hall of the People, and the walls at the Theater's entrance,

painted in dark red, echo the walls of Tiananmen. Introductory articles in field journals register iconic

buildings as outstanding architecture, rather than as mere landmarks.

In contrast to the mass media, field journals are not dominated by introductory articles about

iconic buildings. There is a balance between articles on iconic architecture by foreign architects and

on works by local architects. Introductory articles on works by local architects in field journals use

Feng Ze Yuan Hotel, Beijing, 1994, courtesy of China Architecture Design & Research Group
豐澤園飯店，北京，1994年，中國建築設計研究院提供

approaches similar to those in the mass media, emphasizing the Chinese cultural essence in the

buildings described. Two examples are "Mandarin Palace: a Different Villa Typology,"[89] written by

the project's architect, Rocco Yim, and published in *Time + Architecture* in 2005, and "Plainness and

Overstatement — Interview with Architect Huang Jie of Qintai Grand Theater,"[90] published in *New

Architecture* in 2008. I will not analyze these articles here as the points are already made in the section

"Introductory Articles in the Mass Media."

89   *Time + Architecture*, 2005(06), p.108-113. The title of this article is translated by *Time + Architecture*.
90   *New Architecture*, 2008(02), p.60-61. The title of this article is translated by *New Architecture*.

Cui Kai, courtesy of China Architecture Design & Research Group
崔愷，中國建築設計研究院提供

品時，採納類似的寫作手法，強調所介紹建築物的中國文化特色。於2005年在《時代建築》出版、由嚴迅奇撰寫的《九間堂 — 另類的別墅文化》[89]以及2008年《新建築》出版的《平實與張揚 — 武漢琴台大劇院建築師黃捷訪談》[90]是其中兩個例子。本書不會分析這兩篇文章，因為有關論點已在「大眾傳媒的介紹性文章」部分闡述。

介紹性文章與建築實踐

介紹性文章反映了建築師個人形象的冒起。1980年代毛澤東時期結束，設計院進行改革，部分國家擁有的設計院變成自負盈虧，隨著設計院變成財政自治，建築漸漸變成獨立於政府的學科。1980至1990年代的外國投資者將海外建築師帶來中國，這些海外建築師均由投資一方任命。[91]在1994至1995年，中國的建築界成立了一個註冊制度，中國建築師可以考取專業資格，並建立私營建築師事務所。在1990年代後期，當時中國即將加入世界貿易組織，[92]在中國成立的本地及海外的建築師事務所急速增加。目前，中國擁有國營、但設有半自主單位的設計院、

89　《時代建築》，2005(06), p.108-113
90　《新建築》，2008(02), p.60-61
91　Zhu 2009, p.205
92　中國於2001年加入世界貿易組織。

Introductory Articles and the Practice of Architecture

Introductory articles reflect the emergence of the figures of individual architects. After the end of the Maoist era, design institutes were reformed in the 1980s. Some previously state-owned design institutes became financially autonomous, and with financial independence came more autonomy from state control. Also in the 1980s and 1990s, international investment in design and construction began to bring into China overseas architects appointed by foreign investors.[91] In 1994-5, a registration system was established and architects in China could obtain licenses to set up private practices. In the late 1990s, the number of local and foreign practices increased rapidly as China prepared to join the WTO.[92] At present, there are state-owned design institutes with semi-autonomous units, private ateliers, international architects and "hybrid and shifting combinations among them."[93] Under the market mechanism, architects in China are gaining relative autonomy from state authority in terms of design ideas and financial support.[94] A collective expression of design ideas directed by the state has been replaced by the design visions of individual architects, which may oppose or transcend mainstream conventions. Such individual architects include Cui Kai of state-owned institute China Architecture and Design Research Group, Chang Yungho of private practice Atelier Feichang Jianzhu, Liu Jiakun of Jiakun Architects, Qingyun Ma of MADA s.p.a.m., and others.

Introductory articles also show the fading of the "anti-waste" discourse since 1978 and, more

---

91   Zhu 2009, p.205
92   China joined WTO in 2001.
93   Zhu 2009, p.113
94   Zhu 2009, p.119

私營建築師事務所、國際建築師事務所、以及這幾類建築設計機構的變種或混合體。[93]比較毛澤東時期，當今在市場機制底下，中國的建築師在設計意念及財政上，均取得相對自主性。[94]由政府主導、對設計意念的統一表述被建築師的個人立場取代，而建築師都嘗試反對或超越主流慣例。這類獨立建築師包括歸屬國營的中國建築設計研究院的崔愷、私營建築師事務所非常建築的張永和、家琨建築事務所的劉家琨及馬達思班建築設計事務所的馬清運等。

　　大眾傳媒以及專業期刊的介紹性文章亦反映了自1978年，「反西方」的論述開始逐步減弱，而自1990年後期起，有關造價高昂的地標式建築的論述逐漸興起。1998年以後，特別是當北京於2008年贏得奧運主辦權後，政府大力投資大型公共建築建設、體育設施以及基建，而這些項目的建築師都由國際競圖產生。[95]首個此類比賽是1998至1999年間舉辦的國家大劇院國際競圖，保羅‧安德魯獲委任為國家大劇院的設計師。很多歐洲的明星建築師隨後相繼贏取了政府大力投資的項目的委任設計權，而由他們設計的地標式建築開始陸續在中國出現。自此，地標式建築備受中國傳媒注視。

　　毛澤東時期以後的介紹性文章向讀者展示更多元化的建築論述中的討論話題或對象，讀者可自由參與有關建築的辯論，而大眾傳媒以及專業期刊的介紹性文章均向讀者提供不同資訊，讓他們組成不同意見。

93　Zhu 2009, p.113
94　Zhu 2009, p.119
95　Zhu 2009, p.205.

recently, the rise of discourse on iconic architecture requiring huge investment. From 1998 onwards, especially after Beijing won its bid to host the 2008 Olympic Games, the government invested heavily in large public buildings, sports facilities and infrastructure projects, and architects for these projects were selected through international competitions.[95] The first such competition was held in 1998-9 for the National Grand Theater. The commission was awarded to Paul Andreu. Many European star architects won commissions for such projects and iconic architecture designed by them became available in China. Iconic architecture has now come under the media spotlight.

Introductory articles in the post-Mao era expose the audience to a greater variety of subjects of discourse. The audience has the freedom to participate in debates on architecture, and introductory articles in both the mass media and field journals equip the audience with information to formulate different opinions.

Paul Andreu, courtesy of Paul Maurer
保羅・安德魯，Paul Maurer 提供

95   Zhu 2009, p.205.

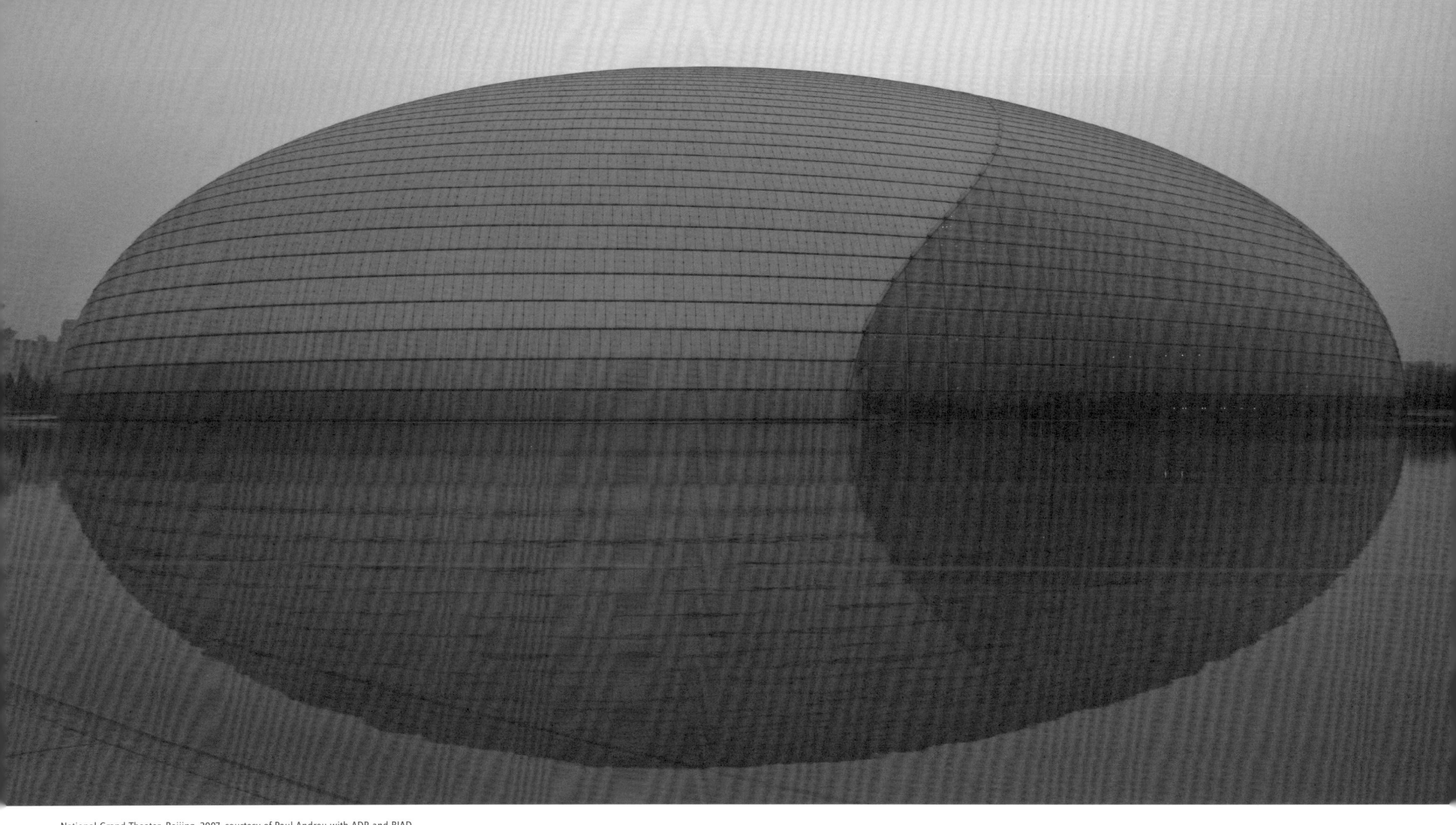

National Grand Theater, Beijing, 2007, courtesy of Paul Andreu with ADP and BIAD
國家大劇院，北京，2007年，保羅・安德魯聯同 ADP 及北京市建築設計研究院提供

COMMENTARIES: EMERGENCE OF DIFFERENT OPINIONS IN THE POST-MAO ERA

Commentaries reflecting different opinions are widely available today. The general public can also respond to these commentaries, and publish their own, much more easily through the internet. There have been two major moments of change with respect to commentaries since 1949 — the late 1970s when the Maoist era ended, and around the millennium with the proliferation of internet use in China.

Commentaries in the Mass Media from 1979 to the Late 1990s

In the late 1970s and early 1980s, with the Maoist era still a recent memory, commentaries on the principles for architecture set by the Maoist government continued to appear in newspapers. The commentaries were not only written by government news agencies and government officials, but also by architectural professionals and columnists. These columnists could not truly be called architectural critics, since their architecture writings were sporadic — the concept of "architectural critic" did not really exist in China at that time.

However, in the commentaries that appeared in the late 1970s and early 1980s, architects and columnists no longer took the principles for architecture literally. They began to question the meanings of such principles and explicitly condemn unilateral views. The shortcomings of the principles were pointed out. In "Aesthetics in Architecture Should be Considered" written by columnist Feng Lifang

"Aesthetics in Architecture Should be Considered," *Guangmin Daily*, 21 May 1980
《光明日報》，《建築應該講究美觀》，1980年5月21日

評論：意見紛陳的後毛澤東時期

　　反映不同意見的評論文章目前於中國大陸廣泛出現。一般大眾也可以比以往更容易透過互聯網回應這些評論。中國的評論文章有兩個重要的改變時刻 ── 1970年代後期，即毛澤東時期結束之時，以及約2000年互聯網在中國全面普及之初。

1979年至90年代後期主流傳媒的評論

　　在1970年代末至1980年代初，亦即毛澤東時期完結後不久，有關毛澤東政府訂立的建築創建方針的評論文章繼續於報章出現。這些文章不單由政府新聞機構及政府官員撰寫，也由建築專業人士及專欄作家撰寫。這些專欄作家並未可以被稱為建築評論家，因為他們創作的建築寫作有限，而更重要的是，當時中國並沒有「建築評論家」的概念。

　　在當時出版的建築評論中，建築師及評論家並未根據字面意義解讀毛澤東政府訂立的建築創建方針。相反地，他們開始質疑這些方針的意思，並明確批評片面的意見。方針一些可能存在的缺點亦被逐一點出。在1980年5月21日《光明日報》刊載、由馮利芳撰寫的《建築應該講究美觀》一文，馮利芳重申並質疑了政府提出的「實用、經濟、在可能條件下注意美觀」方針，指出實用及經濟層面未必一定比美觀重要，而「應該處理好適用、經濟、美觀的辯證關係」。

and published in *Guangmin Daily* on 21 May 1980, Feng reiterates the "functional, economical, and delightful if conditions permit" principle set by the government but questions this principle. He suggests that functional and economical aspects should not necessarily come before aesthetics, and "the dialectic relationship between the meanings of functional, economical and delightful should be dealt with."

Commentaries on buildings after the Maoist era also discouraged reductive judgments, encouraging readers to look at buildings from different perspectives and ask questions about what made a design "good" or "bad." For example, in "Also on the Monotony of Architectural Design" written by architect Gu Mengchao and published in *People's Daily* on 10 April 1989, Gu defends the box-like architecture that was widely described as "monotonous" in the late 1980s. He says architecture should be evaluated both from the perspective of "people with property" and "people without property," suggesting the latter would have higher opinions of this kind of architecture, which could be mass produced and help solve the housing problems of the era. Gu suggests that the "monotonous architectural designs" should not be blindly condemned, but people should ask questions about what the "monotonous designs" were and why they had been created.

In the commentaries that appear in newspapers after the late 1970s, writers present their

毛澤東時期以後的建築評論文章亦反對武斷，鼓勵讀者從不同角度觀察建築，並考慮究竟是甚麼元素斷定建築的「好」與「壞」。例如在1989年4月10日《人民日報》出版、由建築師顧孟潮撰寫的《也談建築的千篇一律》一文，顧孟潮為1980年代流行、被廣泛形容為「千篇一律」的「方盒子」辯護。他指出「方盒子」應該從「有其屋者」及「無房戶」兩個不同的出發點被考慮，指出「有其屋者」及「無房戶」對「方盒子」有兩種截然不同的感情：「『有其屋者』往往冷眼旁觀地評論這些方盒子如何面目可憎；而無房戶則當有了一套現代化的方盒了住宅時，會禁不住熱淚盈眶，他們也曾兩眼圓呼，朝思暮想著有自己的『方盒子』」，因為「方盒子」能大規模、高速度地進行建設，解決當時的住屋問題。顧孟潮指出人們「不能不加分析地盲目排斥『千篇一律』」，而應該討論甚麼是「十篇一律」的設計，而它們又為甚麼會產生。

　　在1970年代末起於報章出現的評論文章中，作者僅代表他們自己的聲音，而並未像毛澤東時期的新聞機構或官員一樣，聲稱自己是讀者意見的代表。1970年代末至1990年代的評論，反映了一場由政府官員、記者、建築專業人士及專欄作家之間有關建築的辯論；不過我們需

own voices instead of claiming to represent the public's views, as government news agencies and government officials did in the Maoist era. The commentaries registered active debates on architecture among government officials, reporters, architectural professionals, and columnists from the late 1970s to the 1990s, but there is no obvious evidence that the general public participated in such debates given that there were few, if any, writings by ordinary people in newspapers. Nonetheless, these commentaries, unlike those of the Maoist era, did open up the subjects discussed for possible debate by avoiding definitive judgments on architectural issues. Writers of the commentaries often took on the task of interpreting architecture for the general public, to equip them with the information to participate in debates about architecture.

Commentaries in Field Journals from 1979 to the Late 1990s

Commentaries in field journals from the late 1970s to the 1990s had a clearer theme than those in the mass media. When Deng Xiaoping announced, in the early 1980s, that China should develop socialism with Chinese characteristics, the question of whether China should also develop new socialist architecture with "Chinese characteristics" arose. Field journals in that period registered a debate about whether modern Chinese architecture should have "Chinese characteristics" and

要留意，這些評論文章並未提供足夠證據，顯示一般大眾也積極參與相關討論，因為這段期間報章只有極少數由大眾撰寫的有關建築的文章。另外，這些評論文章不像毛澤東時期的文章一樣，企圖為有關建築的各個議題下清晰的定案，反而為文章所討論的內容開展辯論的可能性。這些評論的作者也以向大眾闡述他們對建築的理解為己任，為大眾提供參與建築辯論所需的資訊。

1979年至90年代後期專業期刊的評論

從1970年代末至1990年代，專業期刊的評論文章較大眾傳媒的評論文章更主題清晰。當鄧小平於1980年代初宣佈中國要發展有中國特色的社會主義時，有關中國應否發展有「中國特色」的新社會主義建築的議題隨之出現。當時的專業期刊紀錄了有關中國當代建築應否具備中國特色，以及何謂中國特色的辯論。儘管部分較激進的意見在詮釋中國特色時，以外型為基礎，將「大屋頂」及「斗拱」等中國建築結構部分視為展示中國特色的主要元素，並宣稱這些中國元素毫無必要，主流意見卻鼓吹根據西方標準來説，可被視為當代，但同時又富有中國特

discussed the meaning of that term. A few expressed more extreme opinions, interpreting Chinese characteristics based on formal criteria, regarding "big roofs" or "dougong brackets" as major features exemplifying Chinese characteristics, and asserting that these features were totally unnecessary. Most opinions, however, advocated architecture that was both modern in the western sense and possessed Chinese characteristics. "A Discussion on the Slogan 'Socialist Content, National Form' in Architecture"[96] written by architect Ying Ruo and published in *Architectural Journal* in 1981 was one of the few examples arguing against Chinese characteristics. In Ying's view, western buildings such as Centre Pompidou exemplify the modern architecture that Chinese architects should learn from. The author expresses a relatively blind belief in modern western architecture, saying that "beauty lies in true innovation,"[97] and that Centre Pompidou, which "challenged the tradition," is "something that people would love to see, whether its design is good or not."[98] The article condemns the incorporation of Chinese characteristics into architecture, regarding this as an obstacle to the modernization of Chinese architecture.

96   *Architectural Journal*, 1981(02) p.60-63
97   Ying 1981, p.62
98   Ying 1981, p.63

色的建築。1981年於《建築學報》出版，由應若撰寫的《談建築中『社會主義內容，民族形式』的口號》[96]一文，是其中少數反對建築存有中國特色的文章之一。應若視如龐比度中心的西方建築為中國建築師應該學習的當代建築，表現了他對當代西方建築一種相對盲目的信仰：他指出「真正創新就是美」，[97]而「巴黎的龐比度藝術中心，以其新穎的形式正在向傳統挑戰。它設計的好壞姑且不論，但肯定是群眾"喜聞樂見"的。」[98]在文中，將中國特色融入建築被視為妨礙中國建築現代化，備受抨擊。

同時期的其他評論文章卻並未就中國特色提出一個特定的結論，反而鼓勵辯論，並經常提出促請讀者不要「盲目」相信西方當代性的字眼，以打擊片面的意見。這些評論文章的作者主要是建築師，他們一方面承認應該從外國建築師身上學習，另一方面亦肯定中國建築師的專業知識。在1981年出版的《對『談建築中「社會主義內容，民族形式」的口號』的意見》[99] 一

96　《建築學報》，1981(02) p.60-63
97　應若 1981, p.62
98　應若 1981, p.63
99　《建築學報》，1981(12) p.29-31

Fragrant Hill Hotel, Beijing, 1982, courtesy of Pei Cobb Freed & Partners
香山飯店，北京，1982年，Pei Cobb Freed & Partners 提供

Other articles in the same period offer less definitive conclusions about Chinese characteristics, instead encouraging debate. The articles urged the audience not to "blindly" believe in western modernism and discouraged unilateral opinions. Authors of these articles, mostly architects, admitted that they should learn from foreign architects, but also recognized the expertise of Chinese architects. For example, in "Comments on 'A Discussion on the Slogan 'Socialist Content, National Form' in Architecture"[99] published in 1981, architect Wang Dihua criticizes Ying's blind belief in western modern architecture, saying that Chinese architects "have the ability to create Chinese architecture for the new generation."[100] The preface of the first issue of *Huazhong Architecture*, published in 1983 and titled "Construct More New Socialist Architecture with Chinese Characteristics,"[101] admits that Chinese architects should be "humble students" and learn from the west, while at the same time acknowledging that architects in China are "knowledgeable," "important" and "promising."[102] To stimulate debate, instead of stating his arguments directly, the author puts forward questions before

99   *Architectural Journal*, 1981(12) p.29-31
100   Wang 1981, p.30
101   *Huazhong Architecture*, 1983(01), p.7-13
102   Editorial board of *Huazhong Architecture* 1983, p.8

文，建築師汪滌華批評應若盲目崇拜西方建築，指出「中國廣大建築工作者，儘管同遭浩劫耽擱了大好年華，但仍然有志氣有能力，一定能創造出新一代中國的建築。」[100]1983年出版的第一期《華中建築》卷首語，題為《建設更多具有中國特色的社會主義新型建築》，[101]承認中國建築師應該學習西方建築的長處，「願當恭謹的學生」，但「決不作他人之附庸」，並肯定中國建築師的能力：「具有淵博學識和長期實戰經驗的老一輩建築師是新中國建築界的中流砥柱，是引路人，在社會主義建設中鍛鍊成長的中年建築師是可貴的中堅力量，尤其令人欣慰的是：我們開始看到了可畏的中國青年建築師 ── 一代新葩的活力。」[102]為了鼓勵討論，作者並未直接陳述論點，卻運用設問的方法，在發表每一項意見前都先問問題，引發讀者思考。例如在文章的開端，作者便問到「中國的建築創作往何處去？新型建築要不要具有社會主義的『中國特色』？」，[103]以展開文章往後部分的討論。在闡述其意見前，作者又先問「(中國當代建

100　汪滌華 1981, p.30
101　《華中建築》，1983(01), p.7-13
102　《華中建築》編輯部 1983, p.8
103　《華中建築》編輯部 1983, p.7

making his own comments. At the beginning of the article, the author asks, "Does new architecture need to show socialism with 'Chinese characteristics'?"[103] in order to open up discussions in the subsequent part of the piece. The author also asks "What is the main theme [of modern Chinese architecture]?" and "What are [Chinese] characteristics?"[104] before giving his own opinions. Such articles show the willingness of architects to debate important architectural issues, as they sought new directions for development after the end of the Maoist era.

In the 1980s and 1990s, "modern with Chinese characteristics" began to replace "functional, economical, and delightful if conditions permit" as the main criterion for judging buildings, notably reflected in commentaries on I.M. Pei's Fragrant Hill Hotel. The design of Fragrant Hill Hotel began in 1979 and the hotel opened in 1982. The hotel is characterized by each guest room opening onto a courtyard. Pei aimed to develop a distinct "Chinese form of modern architecture that could be adapted, not merely adopted, for diverse building types."[105] Most commentaries on the hotel did not just evaluate the building as an artefact, but also discussed the concepts behind the design. In "An

103 *Huazhong Architecture editorial board* 1983, p.7
104 *Huazhong Architecture editorial board* 1983, p.11
105 Pei Cobb Freed & Partners, http://www.pcfandp.com/a/p/7905/s.html

Interior view, Fragrant Hill Hotel, Beijing, 1982, courtesy of Pei Cobb Freed & Partners
香山飯店室內景觀，北京，1982年，Pei Cobb Freed & Partners 提供

Site plan, Fragrant Hill Hotel, Beijing, 1982, courtesy of Pei Cobb Freed & Partners
香山飯店總平面圖，北京，1982年，Pei Cobb Freed & Partners 提供

築的)主調是甚麼？及（中國）『特色』是甚麼呢？」[104]這些文章反映建築師在毛澤東時期結束後，都樂意參與有關建築的討論，尋找發展的新方向。

在1980至1990年代，「既當代又富中國特色」的新要求取代「實用、經濟、在可能條件下注意美觀」的舊方針，成為判斷建築優劣的主要條件。有關貝聿銘設計的香山飯店的評論可反映這項轉變。香山飯店的設計於1979年開始，而飯店於1982年竣工。香山飯店的特色，是每個客房都面對一個院落。貝聿銘希望設計一個獨特的當代中國建築造型，而此造型不單可以應用，更是適用於不同的建築類型。[105]大多數就香山飯店的評論都並未將香山飯店單單看作一件建築工藝品（artefact），卻討論了建築的背後理念。1981年於《建築學報》刊登、由建築師王天錫撰寫的《香山飯店設計對中國建築創作民族化的探討》[106]一文，引述貝聿銘的設計理念，指香山飯店「以建築圍成的院落做為空間佈局的基本要素，從而使它具有了中國傳統建

104　《華中建築》編輯部1983, p.11
105　貝柯傳建築事務所, http://www.pcfandp.com/a/p/7905/s.html
106　《建築學報》，1981(06), p.13-18

Analysis of the Impact of the Fragrant Hill Hotel Design on Nationalization of China's Architectural Design"[106] written by architect Wang Tianxi and published in *Architectural Journal* in 1981, Pei is quoted explaining that the hotel's design concept is based on the courtyard, one of the most essential elements in Chinese architecture.[107] In "An Analysis of I.M. Pei's Design Thoughts Through Fragrant Hill Hotel"[108] by Gu Mengchao published in *Architectural Journal* in 1983, Gu puts forward a summary of Pei's design ideas as reflected in Fragrant Hill Hotel, saying that Pei's designs were rooted in China, were based on human needs, and echoed with the environment.

The commentaries praised Pei's design for providing a new direction for "nationalization," or the incorporation of Chinese elements into modern Chinese architecture. Both the western elements and the Chinese characteristics of the building were emphasized. In Wang's article, he emphasizes the fact that the plan of the hotel resembles that of a traditional Chinese garden, while describing the atrium of the hotel as an element "always used in the west in recent years."[109] The atrium, a "western"

106 *Architectural Journal,* 1981(06), p.13-18
107 Wang 1981, p.14
108 *Architectural Journal,* 1983(04), p.61-64
109 Wang 1981, p.15-16

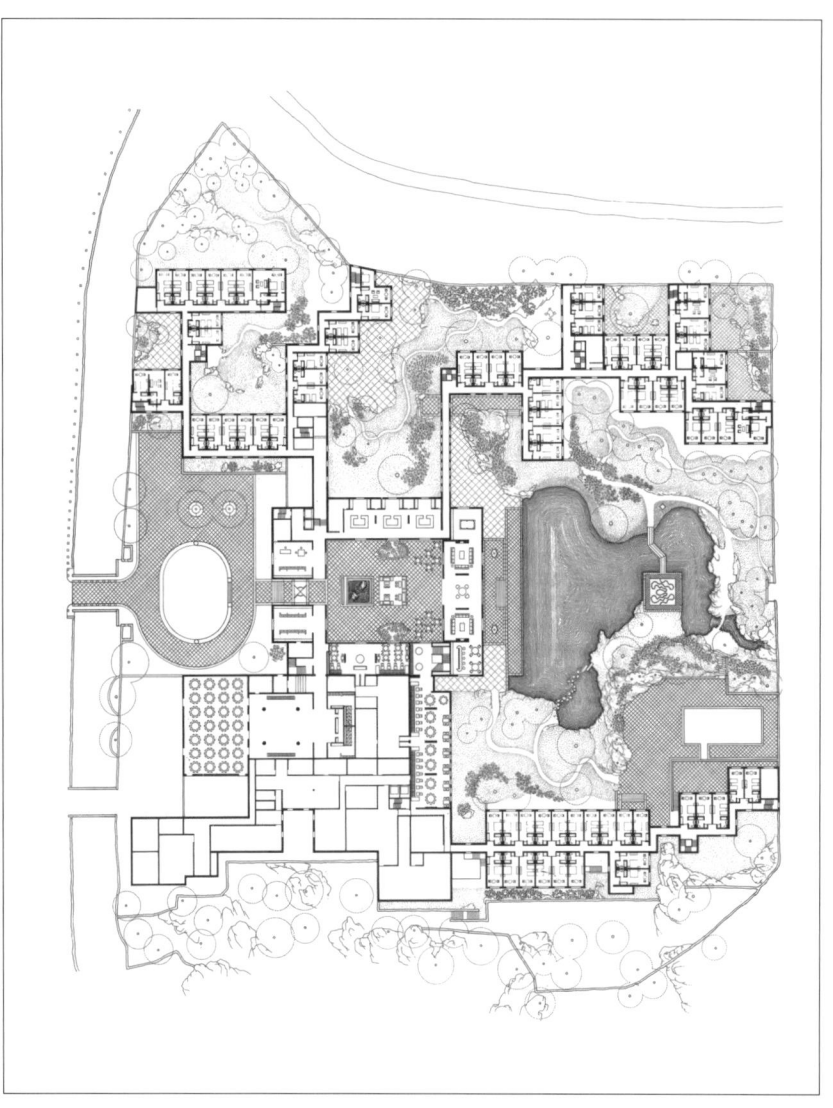

Plan, Fragrant Hill Hotel, Beijing, 1982, courtesy of Pei Cobb Freed & Partners
香山飯店平面圖，北京，1982年，Pei Cobb Freed & Partners 提供

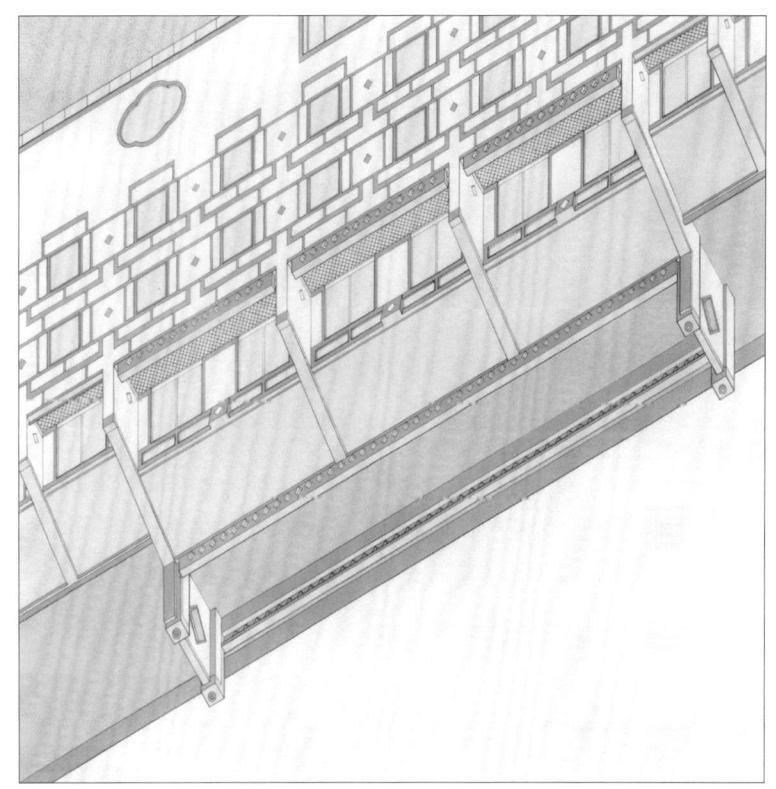

Façade, Fragrant Hill Hotel, Beijing, 1982, courtesy of Pei Cobb Freed & Partners
香山飯店外牆，北京，1982年，Pei Cobb Freed & Partners 提供

築藝術的基本特徵之一」。[107]在1983年《建築學報》出版的《從香山飯店探討貝聿銘的設計思想》[108]一文，作者顧孟潮以香山飯店為例，逐點分析貝聿銘五項主要建築設計思想，包括「歸根」、「環境第一」、「一切服從人」、「刻意傳神」及「重視空間和體形」。

在這些評論中，貝聿銘的設計由於為中國當代建築的「民族化」(nationalization)提供了方向，亦即提供了將中國特色融入當代建築的指引，因而受到高度評價。這些評論均強調香山飯店的西方元素及中國特色。在《香山飯店設計對中國建築創作民族化的探討》一文，王天錫強調香山飯店「平面看上去則儼然類似一個中國古典園林」，而飯店的「四季庭院」，亦即採光頂棚覆蓋著的「院落」，「實際上這是一個近年在西方建築中經常出現的atrium」。[109]這個「西方」元素被形容為「並未使香山飯店因而失去了中國的格調。究其原因，是對稱的四合院式得到了融合，中國的傳統處理手法得到了發展。」[110]在1983年《新建

107 王天錫 1981, p. 14
108 《建築學報》，1983(04), p.61-64
109 王天錫 1981, p.15-16
110 王天錫 1981, p.16

element, is praised for not detracting from the hotel's Chinese characteristics, since it is incorporated into an overall layout based on traditional Chinese gardens.[110] In "Discuss the Modernization and Nationalization in our Country's Architectural Design Through Fragrant Hill Hotel"[111] written by the founder of the architecture department of Huazhong University of Science and Technology, Zhou Buyi, and published in 1983, Fragrant Hill Hotel is said "to have exemplified the spirit of modern architecture as Gropius's design of Bauhaus Dessau has."[112] Zhou also says the hotel differs from Fallingwater by Frank Lloyd Wright only in the sense that it is a Chinese garden hotel,[113] and describes it as "an adequate textbook on modern architecture that should be studied by us [Chinese architects]."[114] There seemed to be a consensus among architects in the 1980s that designing buildings with Chinese essence was a possible route for development of modern Chinese architecture — though the best route for development was yet to be determined.

110 Wang 1981, p.16
111 *New Architecture,* 1983(01), p.17-22
112 Zhou 1983, p.17
113 Ibid.
114 Zhou 1983, p.19

築》出版、華中科技學院建築系創辦人周卜頤撰寫的《從香山飯店談我國建築創作的現代化與民族化》[111]一文,周卜頤將香山飯店形容為「與格羅庇斯設計的著名鮑豪斯校舍一樣富有現代建築精神。」[112]周卜頤亦指香山飯店是「賴特有機建築理論的體現」,「有膾炙人口的流水別墅的情趣,所不同的只是中國式的園林飯店而已」,[113]而香山飯店「儼然是一部完備的現代建築設計的教科書,值得我們(建築師)很多學習,從中得到教益,以提高我們的設計水平。」[114]在1980年代,建築師之間似乎存在一個共識,認為設計有中國神髓的建築是中國當代建築一條可行的發展之路,儘管怎樣才是最佳的發展路向當時仍未有定案。

1990年代末期以後有關地標式建築的辯論

自1990年代末開始,互聯網成為發表評論的普及平台。互聯網上的部分評論專門為網站或博客撰寫,而其他則轉載自報章、雜誌或專業期刊。其中最受歡迎的中國建築網站之一abbs.com.cn

111 《新建築》, 1983(01), p.17-22
112 周卜頤 1983, p.17
113 同上
114 周卜頤 1983, p.19

CCTV Headquarters, Beijing, 2012, Photography by Philippe Ruault, courtesy of OMA
中央電視台新總部大樓，北京，2012
年，Philippe Ruault 攝，OMA 提供

The Debate on Iconic Architecture Since the Late 1990s

Since the late 1990s, the internet has become a popular platform for architectural commentaries. Some commentaries are written specifically for websites or blogs, while others are originally published in newspapers, magazines and field journals. In particular, abbs.com.cn, one of the most widely visited architecture websites in China, publishes articles from each issue of selected field journals. On the other hand, since 2001, *Time + Architecture* has published summaries of discussions taking place on architecture websites.

Commentaries in the mass media reflect debates on several recurring themes centered on the iconic buildings in China designed by foreign star architects. These themes include whether the iconic architecture by foreign architects conflicts with Chinese culture, whether China needs iconic architecture by foreign architects, and how Chinese architects should position themselves under the competition from foreign star architects. In the following section, I will look at the characteristics of these commentaries through the case study of writings about OMA's CCTV Headquarters, which serve as typical examples of commentaries after the millennium.

Commentaries on the CCTV Headquarters, except for those originally published in field journals,

會發表部分專業期刊每期的部分文章。另外，自2001年起，《時代建築》亦開始發表建築網站討論的概要。

於大眾傳媒出現的評論，反映了幾個環繞由外國明星級建築師設計的地標式建築的主題。這些主題包括：外國建築師設計的地標式建築是否與中國文化存有衝突、中國是否需要外國建築師的地標式建築、以及中國建築師在外國明星級建築師的競爭下如何定位等。以下部分將以環繞 OMA 設計的中央電視台新總部大樓的文章，討論於大眾傳媒出現的評論的特點，而這些評論都是自千禧年以來出現的評論文章的典型例子。

除了專業期刊的文章外，有關中央電視台新總部大樓的文章均反映出在中國的普羅大眾之間，存有一場有關地標式建築、卻主題模糊的辯論，而這些辯論甚至很難被判斷為是否與建築有實際關係。在2009年8月，一篇批評中央電視台新總部大樓貌似生殖器官、並指責庫哈斯向中國人開玩笑的文章，在《成都日報》記者雷蕾的個人博客發表；雷蕾在博客並未表明自己是《成都日報》記者，但這篇文章很快紛紛被其他博客及網站轉載。[115]博客是一種相對不甚正式

115 網誌上的這篇文章已被刪除。

illustrate an ambiguity in the public debates on iconic architecture in China — indeed, it is unclear whether such debates are relevant to the architecture. In August 2009, a commentary criticizing the CCTV Headquarters for looking like genitals and accusing Rem Koolhaas of making fun of the Chinese through the design appeared on a Chinese reporter's blog. The blog post was written by Lei Lei, a reporter for *Chengdu Daily*, and published on her personal blog. Lei did not identify herself as a reporter of *Chengdu Daily* in the blog post.[115] The commentary was later widely quoted in other blogs and websites. A blog post is a less formal type of writing and aims to stimulate debate among the general public; in order to engage them, blog posts often refer to buildings according to the informal terms used by the public. The blog post about the CCTV Headquarters refers to the building as "underpants," which is what the general public in China calls it, and uses a conversational tone to engage the public in discussion. In the commentary, the reporter tries to interpret the "meaning" behind the form of the CCTV Headquarters. It seems that in commentaries in China's mass media, identifying the "meaning" of a building's form is equivalent to finding an object that the form resembles, and the meaning associated with that object in turn becomes the "meaning" behind the

115 The blog post has already been deleted.

的寫作種類，旨在鼓勵大眾透過留言參與討論。為鼓勵大眾參與討論，博客的文章通常以大眾普遍使用的不正式詞彙稱呼建築物。例如有關中央電視台新總部大樓的博客與一般大眾一樣，將大樓稱為「大褲衩」。文章亦採納一種較為口語化的語調，鼓勵大眾參與討論。在評論中，記者嘗試詮釋央視大樓外型背後的「意義」。對於中國大眾傳媒，找尋一座建築物的外型的「意義」，彷彿等同於找尋一件與建築物外型相類的物件，並將與這件物件相關的意義視為建築物外型背後的「意義」。例如赫爾佐格與德梅隆 (Herzog & de Meuron) 設計的北京國家體育場，其外型的背後「意義」是「出生」，因為人眾認為體育場的外型像哺育雀鳥的鳥巢一樣。在雷蕾的博客中，中央電視台新總部大樓被詮釋成女性生殖器官，而毗連的電視文化中心則被解讀成男性生殖器官。中央電視台新總部大樓背後的「意義」因此是「性交」。大眾通常都傾向於即時透過留言回應文章，因此他們很多在求證雷蕾的論點以前，便同意了她的意見，並對中央電視台新總部大樓的色情含義感到憤怒，儘管也有讀者持其他意見。閱讀了雷蕾的評論的大眾參與了一場有關中央電視台新總部大樓設計是否色情、以及庫哈斯是否在開中國人玩笑的辯論，而中央電視台新總部大樓的外貌對於建築創建的意義從未被討論，由此可見，這樣的辯論已經與建築脫軌；這場辯論其實是有關民族主義的辯論，卻化妝成與建築相關。

由於博客是相對不正式的寫作種類，博客引述用作支持論點的所謂事實通常都未被引證。雷蕾的評論引起全國注意，促使《青年周末》記者嘗試引證博客聲稱足以證明中央電視台新總部大樓設計色情的所謂「事實」，而這些「事實」後來都被證實為捏造。[116]庫哈斯亦發表聲明，否認有關設計的色情連繫，而這張聲明亦被翻譯成中文，於雜誌刊登。換言之，在網上有關中央電視台新總部大樓的討論一直以錯誤的資料為基礎，而網上持續進行的辯論究竟是否與建築創建有關，實在值得商榷。

自1990年代末開始，建築評論亦於報章副刊及雜誌的專欄出現，而評論家的角色亦開始成形。《新民晚報》的「建築物語」一欄是有關建築的定期專欄；《南方都市報》的「城事」、《新民晚報》的「夜光杯」及《羊城晚報》的「晚會」均經常刊登建築評論。這些專欄出不同作者撰寫，但定期撰寫建築評論的個別著名建築評論家似乎並未出現。個別評論家及建築師亦會接受報章及雜誌訪問，發表意見。除此以外，節錄自專業期刊的評論亦會在報章及雜誌上刊登。儘管這些評論的意見比博客的意見更為細緻，但牽涉的辯論仍以外國建築師設

116　《央視大樓的『色情門』假象》，《青年周末》，2009年8月27日，Vol.179

CCTV Headquarters, Beijing, 2012,
courtesy of OMA and Jim Gourley
中央電視台新總部大樓，北京，2012年，
OMA 及 Jim Gourley 提供

form. For example, the "meaning" behind the form of the National Stadium by Herzog & de Meuron is "birth," because the form of the building is thought to resemble a bird's nest where eggs are hatched. In the blog post written by Lei Lei, the main tower of the CCTV Headquarters is interpreted to represent the female genitals, with the Television Cultural Center (TVCC) as the male genitals. The "meaning" behind the form of the CCTV Headquarters is thus "having sex." The general public responded to the commentary, often spontaneously, by leaving comments. Many agreed with Lei Lei's opinions and were furious, while some held different views. The public therefore engaged in a debate on whether the CCTV Headquarters was a pornographic design, and whether Koolhaas was making fun of the Chinese. The implications of the building for architecture design and construction were never discussed. The debate, as it deviated from architecture, became a debate on nationalism masquerading as one on architecture.

As blog posts are an informal type of writing, the so-called facts described in blog posts, and on which opinions are based, are often not verified. The popularity of the blog post about the CCTV Headquarters led the magazine *Y Weekend* to verify the "facts" that the post claimed were proof that

計的地標式建築是否與中國文化相融為焦點，而非有關地標式建築對中國建築創建的意義。換言之，地標式建築如何影響城市，以及如何影響中國建築物的創建均未被討論。這些評論通常強調建築由外國建築師設計，例如2009年3月16日於《羊城晚報》出版的《中國莫成妖魔鬼怪式建築實驗場》，訪問了「清華大學建築學院教授、著名建築大師及建築評論家彭培根」，在訪問中，彭培根不斷提及「外國建築師」或「洋建築大師」這些詞彙，批評「最近10年中，許多外國建築師在中國設計了很多一味追求視覺刺激和『妖魔鬼怪一般』的建築物。」這類攻擊外國建築師的評論文章亦作了很多既有假設，例如：所有在中國的建築都應該反映中國文化、外國建築師將中國當作「實驗場」、以及外國建築師不懂中國文化等。在2005年《時代建築》出版、同濟大學教授鄭時齡撰寫的《境外建築師在中國的實驗與中國建築師的邊緣化》[117]一文，鄭時齡指出「中國已經成為他們（境外建築師）設計思想的實驗室，甚至奇特思想的實驗室。」同樣地，彭培根亦在《中國莫成妖魔鬼怪式建築實驗場》一文多次提及「實驗場」的字眼。另外，鄭時齡及彭培根兩人都批評了中央電視台新總部大樓的設計違反了結構原則，並

117 《時代建築》，2005(01)，p.34-35

the CCTV Headquarters is a pornographic design, and it concluded that they had been fabricated.[116] Koolhaas also issued a statement denying the pornographic associations and his statement was translated and published in the magazine. It is thus doubtful whether the internet debate on the CCTV Headquarters, based on such misinformation, was relevant to the architecture at all.

Since the late 1990s, commentaries have also appeared in regular columns in the features sections of newspapers and magazines and the figure of the architecture critic has begun to emerge. "Jianzhu Wuyu" of *Xinmen Evening News* is a regular column on architecture. "Chengshi," "Yeguangbei," and "Wanhui," of *Southern Metropolis Daily*, *Xinmen Evening News*, and *Yangcheng Evening News*, respectively, are examples of columns that often publish commentaries on architecture. These columns are contributed by various authors, but it seems that prominent individual architecture critics who contribute articles regularly cannot yet be identified. Critics and architects are also interviewed and their opinions are published in the media. Excerpts from field journals are published in newspapers and magazines as well. While the opinions in these commentaries are more sophisticated than those in the blog posts, the debates recorded in these commentaries still tend to focus on whether

116 "Illusions About CCTV's 'Pornographic Gate'," *Y Weekend* 27, August 2009, Vol.179

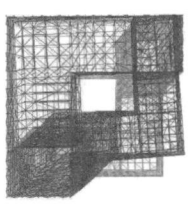
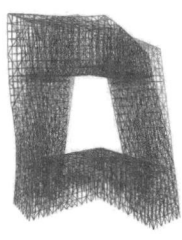

Mode shapes, CCTV Headquarters,
Beijing, 2012, courtesy of OMA
中央電視台新總部大樓剖外形輪廓,
北京,2012年,OMA 提供

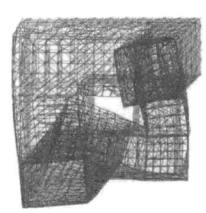

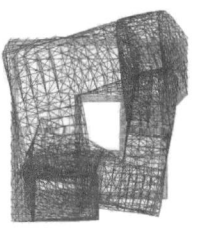
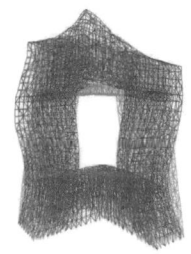

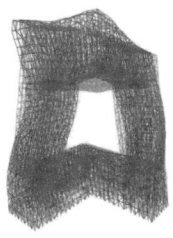
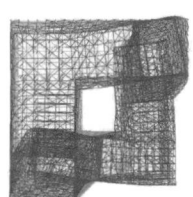

指責庫哈斯將大樓的建造當作一項實驗。[118]在2003年《新建築》出版、由浙江大學建築及美術歷史學家河清撰寫的《應當絞死建築師？ — 中央電視台新大樓中標建築方案質疑》[119]一文,河清將「楞」的中央電視台新總部大樓與「中和」的文化精神對照,指「中和」強調平衡與和諧,而「歪七斜八」的中央電視台新總部大樓「與中國風水學說強調建築與自然環境相和諧的思想截然相悖,不符合中國人的審美」,而「這次中央電視台新大樓的建築方案,不僅『楞』,而且『歪』,是一個『歪門』,酷似一個曲著頭、兩腳癱地的小兒麻痺症患者!」[120]上述的評論往往強調東方文化的獨特概念,暗指外國建築師在設計中未曾、甚至沒有能力考慮這些概念。1980年代盛行的建築評論關注何謂「中國特色」,但自1990年代末開始,建築評論並未反映出有關「中國文化」的意思的討論,而地標式建築為中國文化帶來新意義的這種可能性似乎被全盤否定。儘管理論上,評論最低限度也應該開展有關外國建築師的設計,是否符合

118 彭培根於文中並未直接點出他所批評的大樓是哪一座,但從文中描述,讀者可以估計他談及的正是中央電視台新總部大樓。
119 《新建築》,2003(05), p.13-15
120 河清 2003, p.14

iconic architecture by foreign architects fits with Chinese culture, instead of the implications of iconic architecture for China's architectural design and construction. In other words, there is little discussion of how the iconic architecture intervenes in the city and affects the production of new architecture in China. Such commentaries often discuss the iconic buildings with emphasis on the fact that they were designed by foreign architects. For example, "China Should Not be the Laboratory for Monster-Like Architecture," an interview with Peng Peikeng, a professor of architecture at Tsinghua University, published in *Yangcheng Evening News* on 16 March 2009, incessantly uses the term "foreign architects" and criticizes the trend in the past ten years to have "foreign architects" design "monster-like" architecture in China. Such commentaries make implicit assumptions, such as: all architecture in China should reflect Chinese culture; the foreign architects are treating China as "laboratory"; and foreign architects do not understand Chinese culture. In "Practice of Foreign Architects in China and De-Centering of Chinese Architects"[117] published in *Time + Architecture* in 2005 and written by Tongji University professor Zheng Shiling, Zheng says "China has become their [foreign architects'] laboratory for design thoughts, or even weird thoughts." Peng shares the same opinion, as illustrated by his

117   *Time + Architecture*, 2005(01), p.34-35. The title of the article was translated by *Time + Architecture*.

Guangzhou Opera House, Guangzhou,
2010, Photography by Sylvia Chan
廣州歌劇院，廣州，2010年，
陳曼霞攝

中國文化的辯論，但種種既定的假設均堵塞了這種辯論，並只能導致外國建築師的設計並不反映中國文化這項單向的討論結果。上述這些評論因此未能帶來有關中國的地標式建築如何影響建築創建的真正討論。

　　儘管報章及雜誌的大部分評論似乎都未能反映對於建築創建的發展有幫助的討論，以建築專業人士為對象的專業期刊及網站卻有刊登較細膩的文章；這些文章多由於文化大革命後接受教育，或曾於國外接受教育的建築師撰寫，而這些文章都較能引起可以啟發建築創建的討論。以北京為基地的「自由建築報道」網站(far2000.com)及以上海為基地的abbs.com.cn是中國兩個最受歡迎的建築網站之一，這兩個網站都刊載從不同角度討論地標式建築的文章。專業期刊及建築網站同樣發表有關中央電視台新總部人樓的文章，但這些文章並不強調人樓與中國文化的關係或欠缺關係，卻探討了衍生該設計的背後理論，以及建築物對城市的影響。由曾於國外受教育的建築師朱濤撰寫的《大躍進 — 讀解庫哈斯的 CCTV 新總部大樓》一文曾於《新建築》、《南方周末》及 abbs.com.cn 刊登。[121]朱濤於美國哥倫比亞大學取得建築碩士，

121　《新建築》，2003(05)；《南方周末》，2003年4月3日

frequent use of the term "laboratory" in the interview. Both Zheng and Peng[118] criticize the design of the CCTV Headquarters as being against structural principles, and accuse Koolhaas of treating the construction of the building as an experiment. In "The Architects Should be Strangled? — Questioning the Winning Tender of CCTV New Headquarters"[119] written by Zhejiang University art and architecture historian He Qing and published in *New Architecture* in 2003, He contrasts the "weird" design of the CCTV Headquarters with "the doctrine of the mean," a traditional Chinese concept which emphasizes balance and harmony, and accuses Koolhaas's design of contradicting the concept of feng shui.[120] Emphasizing the unique concepts of eastern culture is a way of implying that foreign architects do not or cannot take into consideration such concepts in their designs. Unlike the 1980s, when there was a debate on the meaning of "Chinese characteristics," commentaries since the late 1990s do not reflect a discussion about the meaning of "Chinese culture." The possibility that iconic architecture can give a new meaning to Chinese culture seems to have been ruled out. While the commentaries are supposed to at least open up debate on whether iconic buildings designed by foreign architects fit with Chinese culture, such implicit assumptions actually close off debate, leading invariably to the conclusion that iconic architecture by foreign architects does not reflect Chinese culture. Such commentaries therefore have not led to genuine debate on iconic architecture in China.

Commentaries in newspapers and magazines seldom seem to register debates that would benefit architecture design and construction. However, more sophisticated writings which could stimulate a debate that might inform architecture are available in field journals and websites targeting professionals. These articles are often written by architects who were trained after the Cultural Revolution and studied abroad. *Free Architecture Report* (far2000.com), based in Beijing, and abbs. com.cn, based in Shanghai, are two of the most popular architecture websites in China, and discuss iconic architecture from different perspectives. Both field journals and the websites, for example, offer commentaries on the CCTV Headquarters that do not emphasize the building's relation or lack of relation with Chinese culture, but discuss the theories that led to the design and the possible effects of the building on the city. "Great Leap Forward – Reading of Koolhaas's Design of CCTV New

---

118 Peng did not directly mention the CCTV Headquarters in the article, but the building could be identified by implication.
119 *New Architecture*, 2003(05), p.13-15. The title of the article was translated by *New Architecture*.
120 He 2003, p.14

於中國執業七年後，於2002年報讀該校的博士課程。在文中，朱濤批評「被庫哈斯央視總部大樓的『怪相』激怒」的「內因是那些被激怒的人『少見多怪』。他們多是持一種衰老的心態，表面上聲稱不喜歡『招搖』的東西，偏好『寧靜致遠』，實際上是他們的眼光早已被周遭充斥的平庸大樓、甜媚的建築裝飾物給毀了。」朱濤沒有企圖在中央電視台新總部大樓找出反映中國文化的元素，但分析了該設計在中國的環境中的重要性。他嘗試以展示其對西方當代建築的專業知識，建立其可信性，將中央電視台新總部大樓與眾多西方例子比較，包括1992年美國建築師彼德‧埃森曼 (Peter Eisenman) 為柏林設計的 Max Reinhardt Haus，以及原広司設計的梅田天空之城，論述庫哈斯將兩座大樓在空中相連接，其實並非前無古人。朱濤提出中央電視台新總部大樓的設計對於中國有一項特殊意義，因為它反映出中國「不僅要現代，更重要的是要顯得現代」，指出中央電視台新總部大樓與中國的關係正在於大廈是中國「大躍進」的產物，顯示「我們要向全世界顯示出我們的富裕和強大、前衛和開放。」朱濤的評論展現了中國較年輕

Headquarters" written by architect Zhu Tao, who has been educated overseas, was published in *New Architecture*, abbs.com.cn, and *Southern Weekly*.[121] Zhu Tao received his Master of Architecture degree from Columbia University and enrolled in its PhD program in 2002 after practicing in China for seven years. In the article, Zhu criticizes those angered by the CCTV Headquarters design as having narrow minds and "aged thoughts." He says their abilities to make fair judgments about architecture have been destroyed by the banal buildings abundant in China. Zhu does not attempt to identify elements that reflect Chinese culture in the CCTV Headquarters, but analyzes the significance of the design in the context of China and tries to establish his credibility by displaying expert knowledge of western modern architecture. He compares the CCTV Headquarters with examples such as Peter Eisenman's Max Reinhardt Haus and Hiroshi Hara's Umeda Sky Building to illustrate that Koolhaas's design, connecting two leaning towers, is not ground-breaking, but he suggests that the design has a unique meaning for China because it symbolizes China's desire not only to be modern but also to "look modern." He points out that the relationship between the CCTV Headquarters and China lies in the status of the building as a product of a "Great Leap Forward" — the rapid development of China and the concomitant desire to show wealth and power. Zhu's article is an example of commentaries that show the relatively open mind of the younger generation of architects towards China's iconic architecture and their attempt to analyze its implications. These architects also use field journals and websites as their own discursive spaces to publish commentaries that inform theories on architecture, which in turn inform architectural design and construction. On Zhu's blog, for example, there are commentaries on the meaning of modernism in architecture and on civic architecture — all in the context of China (http://blog.sina.com.cn/zhutaoarchitect). These commentaries attempt to open up the possibility of audience participation in debates on architecture. Websites with these commentaries are mostly visited by architecture students and young professionals in the field, who often respond to the writings with their own comments.

---

121 *New Architecture*, 2003(05); *Southern Weekly*, 3 April 2003. The title of the article was translated by *New Architecture*.

一代建築師對於地標式建築持相對開放的態度，而他們也企圖分析外國建築師的地標式建築對中國城市及中國建築創建的影響。這些建築師也使用專業期刊及網站作為平台，發表評論文章，企圖啟發建築理論，從而也啟發建築的創建。例如建築師朱濤的博客http://blog.sina.com.cn/zhutaoarchitect中討論關於建築當代性、公民建築等的評論文章，都以中國為背景。這些評論文章讓讀者有機會參加有關建築創建的討論。這些網站的讀者通常是建築系學生或年青的建築專業人士，而他們也會透過留言回應文章。

ARCHITECTURE AND PUBLIC OPINION: MORE THAN A CHINESE INTERPRETATION

Architecture writings, in particular commentaries, record the changes in the discourse on architecture. While we are aware of the fact that this discourse reflects changes in architecture design and construction, we should also ask the larger question of how public opinions formed in the discourse could in turn affect architecture design and construction. Public opinions, in general, are understood as opinions of the general public evolved through rational-critical debates. Jürgen Habermas maintains that the general public can participate in the formation of objective knowledge once they have reached a condition of absolutely free and unlimited debate to form public opinions. He envisions "a new world brought about by criticism, clear thinking, and straight talking."[122] Applying Habermas's concept on public opinions to the field of architecture, if the general public could engage in free and unlimited debate on architecture, they could participate in the formulation of objective knowledge which would inform design and construction, even without receiving specific architectural training. Such debates could be reflected in architecture writings. However, based on my analysis of architecture writings in China since 1949, I would argue that the freedom to participate in debates provides a necessary, but not sufficient, condition for the general public to formulate public opinions and thus objective knowledge on architecture — if freedom is understood in the sense of freedom of speech and the freedom to form opinions without limitation or manipulation by the government.

While in the Maoist era debates on architecture were manipulated by the government, the general public gained freedom to participate in debates on architecture with the end of the Maoist regime. Introductory articles since the late 1970s provide various topics of discourse on architecture, and commentaries after the Maoist era register the freedom to express different views on issues related to architecture. However, in commentaries and responses to the commentaries, particularly those on the internet, participation in the debates relevant to architecture design and construction is mostly limited to architectural professionals. The general public either do not respond to opinions expressed in the commentaries, or they merely indicate simple agreement or disagreement with such opinions, without formulating their own. In *Words Between Spaces: Buildings and Language*, Thomas A. Markus questions the possibility of the general public's participation in the discourse on architecture:

> [If] buildings exist in discourse before they exist in physical reality, and if, after their construction, their meaning is ongoingly interpreted through discourse, it becomes a matter of consequence whose discourse we are dealing with, and conversely, whose voices we never hear. Typically, we are dealing with the discourse of authorities – professional, institutional, economic, political. Their discourse may be "enlightened," "progressive," "utopian," "egalitarian," "radical;" but to the extent they retain a monopoly on the definition of those concepts, speaking for and about others, not to them and not with them, their discourse both reflects and reproduces their authority and power.[123]

122 Schwarting 1985, p.96

123 Markus 2002, p.92

建築與公眾意見：跨越中國式的闡述

建築寫作，尤其是評論，反映了建築論述的改變，而建築論述又反映建築創建的變化。在透過建築論述了解建築創建的轉變以外，我們亦應該討論一個更廣泛的問題：在論述中形成的公眾意見，如何影響建築創建？公眾意見泛指公眾在理智及具批判性的討論下漸漸產生的意見。尤爾根‧哈伯瑪斯 (Jürgen Habermas) 認為，公眾一旦擁有權利及條件參與絕對自由及無規限的討論，形成公眾意見，他們就可以參與創造客觀知識，而他的願景，是「一個由評論、清晰思維、直接表達帶來的新世界」。[122]如果將哈伯瑪斯的概念套用於建築領域，我們可以說，未曾受過建築專業教育的大眾一旦可以參與自由及沒有規限的建築辯論，他們就可參與創造客觀的建築知識，而這些知識亦可啟發建築創建。換言之，如果大眾可以參與自由及無限制的討論，他們就可影響建築創建，而這些討論都可以透過建築寫作反映。不過，正如自1949年以來中國的建築寫作所反映，讓大眾自由參與討論，亦即讓大眾享有言論自由，在不受政府限制或操控的情況下發表意見，只提供必要而並非足夠的條件，讓大眾產生公眾意見以至客觀的建築知識。

在毛澤東時期，政府透過本書上述的不同建築寫作操控建築辯論；大眾隨著毛澤東時期的結束，漸漸得到參與建築辯論的自由。1970年代以後的介紹性文章為建築論述提供多個題材，而毛澤東時期以後的評論反映了提出不同意見的自由。不過，正如評論及有關回應所反映（特別是互聯網上的），能自由、無限制地參與有關建築創建討論的人士，通常僅限於建築專業人士。大眾要麼不回應於評論發表的意見，要麼僅表示同意或不同意這些意見，卻沒有闡明自己的意見。在《字裡行間：建築及語言》一書，托瑪斯‧馬庫斯質疑大眾參與建築論述、從而參與建築創建的可能性：

[如果] 建築物在實際環境出現之前是先在論述出現，而如果在它們建成以後，它們的意義會透過論述被不斷闡譯，那麼最重要的是誰人有機會發聲，以及相反地，誰人的聲音永遠不被聽到。通常我們聽到的都是權威的論述 ── 專業、學院、經濟、政治的論述。他們的論述可以是「知性的」、「革新的」、「烏托邦的」、「平等主義的」或「激進的」；不過他們壟斷了這些概念的定義，只是為他人說話或討論他人，但不是對他人說話或與他人說話，他們的論述既反映出、也重新了他們的權威及權力。[123]

---

122 Schwarting 1985, p.96

123 Markus 2002, p.92

The general public, though having freedom of speech in the sense that their views are not manipulated by the government, are not necessarily able to participate in a discourse on architecture or formulate opinions that could lead to the development of objective knowledge, which in turn would influence architecture. The general public, having no specific training in architecture, are in a way excluded from the discourse, which is dominated by architectural professionals, who have the knowledge and power to define it. The general public depend on architectural professionals to interpret architecture for them and to equip them with the knowledge to participate in debates on architecture. Habermas's view that the general public could formulate opinions and participate in the formation of objective knowledge once they can express their views in free and unlimited debates thus does not seem to apply to the field of architecture. Freedom is not the key in this case. Public opinions that could influence architecture can only be formed by people who also have the knowledge to help define the discourse on architecture, or at least to understand the arguments in the discourse, enabling them to respond to arguments and participate in the discussion.

In 1837, English architect and writer Joseph Gwilt stated that the role of the critic is to instruct the public in the principles of architectural taste.[124] In 1968, Hugh Casson said the layman normally takes only a superficial interest in architecture writings and that architectural journalism is written largely for architects.[125] In 2002, Thomas A. Markus said journalists who write about buildings see it as part of their function to educate public taste, and the opinions of "a well-informed and experienced judge" are intended to influence the judgments of less well-informed people.[126] It seems that this holds true, at present, not only in China, where freedom of speech is a relatively new concept, but also in countries where people are well-accustomed to freedom of speech. Architecture writings, instead of serving as a platform for the general public to participate in debates and formulate opinions, remain largely educational, serving the role of improving public taste. The general public, though enjoying freedom of speech, do not seem to be participating in the discourse on architecture. However, while the general public in China still do not seem to be able to influence architecture by taking part in the architectural discourse, the significance of the emergence of freedom of speech in the discourse on architecture since the end of the Maoist era should not be underestimated. The general public in China have the right to voice their opinions on architecture and, like their counterparts in other countries, to give

124 Gwilt 1837, p.ix
125 Casson 1968, p.258
126 Markus 2002, p.95

換言之，大眾儘管擁有言論自由，未被政府操控，他們也不一定可以參與建築論述，並闡明公眾意見，創造可能影響建築創建的客觀知識。簡單來說，沒有受過建築專業訓練的大眾某程度上是被排除在由建築專業人士支配的建築論述之外，因為只有這些專業人士有知識及權力去定義這個論述。大眾依賴建築專業人士向他們解釋建築，賦予他們參與建築辯論所需的知識。哈伯瑪斯認為大眾一旦可以自由及無限制地表達意見，就可以闡明公眾意見，並參與創造客觀知識的這個想法，似乎未能應用於建築領域。在建築領域，自由並不是關鍵。只有不單擁有言論自由，同時也擁有知識去定義建築論述的人士，又或最起碼明白論述中的論點、從而可以回應論點及參與討論的人士，才可以創造有機會影響建築創建的公眾意見。

1837年，英國建築師及作家喬布斯‧格威爾特 (Joseph Gwilt) 指出評論家的工作是提出方針，指引大眾建立建築品味。[124]1968年，休‧卡森指門外漢通常對於建築寫作只有表面興趣，而建築新聞多為建築師而寫。[125]2002年，托瑪斯‧馬庫斯指出撰寫建築文章的記者視教育公眾，提升其品味為他們的任務之一，而「一個知情及有經驗的評判」的意見應該影響一般大眾的意見。[126]這個說法似乎可以綜合目前建築傳媒的現況，既可套用在言論自由仍然是相對新概念的中國，也可套用在慣於享有言論自由的國家。建築寫作並非讓一般大眾參與辯論、從而闡述公眾意見的平台；建築寫作反而擔當起教育大眾、改善公眾品味的角色。大眾儘管享有言論自由，但他們似乎並未透過參與建築論述影響建築創建。儘管目前，中國的大眾似乎仍未能透過參與建築論述而參與建築創建，自毛澤東時期結束以後在建築論述出現的言論自由及其重要性仍不可被忽視。中國的大眾有權利表述他們對於建築的意見，與其他國家的大眾一樣，他們終於有機會影響建築創建。

124 Gwilt 1837, p.ix
125 Casson 1968, p.258
126 Markus 2002, p.95

opinions that could influence architectural design and construction.

The general public's opinions could introduce diversity to the discourse on architecture, which is currently dominated by architectural professionals. I would argue that, in China or elsewhere, whether the general public will take the initiative to participate in the discourse on architecture hinges on whether architectural professionals, rather than monopolizing the discourse on architecture and putting themselves in the role of "educating" the general public, would instead assure the public that they have sufficient knowledge to form opinions, and encourage the public to participate in architecture debates. Architectural professionals have a responsibility to "speak to" and "speak with" the general public, not just to "speak for" them. Architecture is not an architect's personal icon. Architecture is not an artwork in a private gallery. Architecture is not an ivory tower, without access for the general public. The general public's opinions matter. They are the ones who live in architecture. Perhaps they can also have a role in architectural design and construction.

大眾的意見可以為目前被建築專業人士壟斷的建築論述帶來多樣性。我認為在中國以至其他地方，大眾會否主動參與建築論述繫於建築專業人士是否願意肯定大眾擁有足以讓他們形成大眾意見的知識，並鼓勵他們參與建築討論，而非壟斷建築論述，佔據「教育」大眾的位置。建築專業人士有責任「向公眾說話」及「與公眾說話」，而非僅「為公眾說話」。建築不是建築師的個人標誌；建築不是私人畫廊的藝術品；建築不是公眾止步的象牙塔 ── 大眾的意見應該受重視。他們是建築最終的使用者，或許他們也應該在建築創建扮演一個角色。

TITLES OF PUBLICATIONS AND ARTICLES ANALYZED
參考期刊及文章

Field Journals studied 參考專業期刊

Architectural Journal	《建築學報》
Bulletin of the Society for Research in Chinese Architecture	《中國營造學社匯刊》
Die Architektur	《新建築》
Domus China	《Domus 國際中文版》
Huazhong Architecture	《華中建築》
New Architecture	《新建築》
Time + Architecture	《時代建築》
The Builder	《建築月刊》
The Chinese Architect	《中國建築》
World Architecture	《世界建築》

Publications in the mass media studied 大眾傳媒參考期刊

di	《設計新潮》
Beijing Evening News	《北京晚報》
Chutian Metropolis Daily	《楚天都市報》
Guangzhou Daily	《廣州日報》
People's Daily	《人民日報》
Qilu Evening News	《齊魯晚報》
Southern Metropolis Daily	《南方都市報》
The Outlook Magazine	《新視線》
Vision	《Vision 青年視覺》
Xinmin Evening News	《新民晚報》
Yangcheng Evening News	《羊城晚報》
Yangzi Evening News	《揚子晚報》
Y Weekend	《青年周末》

ARTICLES IN PUBLICATIONS IN MASS MEDIA ANALYZED 被分析的大眾傳媒的文章

(in order of appearance in the book 按在本書的出現次序)

8 March 1956 1956年3月8日	Xinhua News Agency 新華社	"State Construction Committee Held the National Infrastructure Congress and Discussed the Preliminary Strategies and Basic Measures for Design, Architecture, and City Development," *People's Daily* 《國家建設委員會召開全國基本建設會議 — 討論了設計、建築、城市建設工作初步規劃和基本措施》，《人民日報》
10 October 1956 1956年10月10日	Lai, Jifa 賴際發	"Increase the New Types of Construction Materials Available," *People's Daily* 《大力增加建築材料新品種》，《人民日報》
8 May 1955 1955年5月8日	Wang, Jiqi 汪季琦	"My Faults in My Design Leadership Work," *People's Daily* 《我在領導設計工作中的錯誤》，《人民日報》
27 August 1955 1955年8月27日	Shandong Province Architecture and Construction Studio 山東省建築工程設計室	"We Designed Classrooms That Are Economical and Functional," *People's Daily* 《我們設計了既經濟又適用的教室》，《人民日報》
18 September 1955 1955年9月18日	Yan, Zixiang 閻子祥	"We Have Made New Standard Designs," *People's Daily* 《我們完成了新的標準設計》，《人民日報》
20 June 1954 1954年6月20日		"Capital Theater Construction Commences," *People's Daily* 《首都劇場開工興建》，《人民日報》
10 April 1964 1964年4月10日		"Fangua Nong Residential Design is Relatively Practical," *Wenhui Bao* 《蕃瓜弄住宅設計做到比較切合實際》，《文匯報》
28 March 1955 1955年3月28日		"Against the Wasteful Practice in Architectural Production," *People's Daily* 《反對建築中的浪費現象》，《人民日報》
23 April 1955 1955年4月23日	Ma, Haoran 馬浩然	"Problems With the Design of the Capital Theater," *People's Daily* 《首都劇場設計中存在的問題》，《人民日報 》
4 May 1974 1974年5月4日	Department of Architecture, Tongji University 同濟大學 "五‧七" 公社建築學專業黨支部	"A Typical 'Western and Weird' Architectural Design, " *Liberation Daily* 《一個『又洋又怪』的建築設計典型》，《解放日報》
29 September 1979 1979年9月29日	Huo, Cunfu 火存福	"The Song of an Expert in Traditional Chinese Architecture – an Interview With Tongji University Professor Chen Congzhou," *Wenhui Bao* 《古建築家之歌 — 訪同濟大學教授陳從周》，《文匯報》
8 November 1982 1982年11月8日	Ji, Honggeng 計泓賡	"I.M. Pei's 'New Chapter of Music,'" *People's Daily* 《貝聿銘的『新樂章』》，《人民日報》

18 September 2007 2007年9月18日	Lai, Renqiong, Yan, Xiaomin 賴仁瓊，閻曉明	"An Interpretation of National Grand Theater," *People's Daily* 《解讀國家大劇院》，《人民日報》
17 July 2006 2006年7月17日	Zhou, Xiaoying 周曉英	"The Legendary Female Architect From Baghdad Zaha," *Xinmin Evening News* 《來自巴格達的傳奇女建築師扎哈》，《新民晚報》
24 April 2010 2010年4月24日	Jian, Ye 金葉	"Father of 'Rose of Desert': a Delirious Dreamer," *Guangzhou Daily* 《『沙漠玫瑰』之父：瘋狂幻想家》，《廣州日報》
27 August 2009 2009年8月27日	Xie, Zhe, Jiang, Yuting 謝哲，蔣玉婷	"Traditional Chinese Music Staged in Modern Architecture," *Yangcheng Evening News* 《現代建築上演絲竹雅韻》，《羊城晚報》
21 May 1980 1980年5月21日	Feng, Lifang 馮利芳	"Aesthetics in Architecture Should be Considered," *Guangmin Daily* 《建築應該講究美觀》，《光明日報》
10 April 1989 1989年4月10日	Gu, Mengchao 顧孟潮	"Also on Monotony of Architectural Design," *People's Daily* 《也談建築的千篇一律》，《人民日報》
August 2009 2009年8月	Lei, Lei 雷蕾	"Designer of Underpants Openly Admits: CCTV Headquarters is a Pornographic Joke" 《大褲衩設計師公開承認：央視大樓是色情玩笑》
27 August 2009 2009年8月27日	Zhang, Wei 張薇	"Illusions About CCTV's 'Pornographic Gate'," *Y Weekend* Vol.179 《央視大樓的『色情門』假象》，《青年周末》Vol. 179
16 March 2009 2009年3月16日	Lei, Cheng 雷成	"China Should Not be the Laboratory of Monster-Like Architecture," *Yangcheng Evening News* 《中國莫成妖魔鬼怪式建築實驗場》，《羊城晚報》

ARTICLES IN FIELD JOURNALS ANALYZED 被分析的專業期刊文章

(in order of appearance in the book 按在本書的出現次序)

Year	Author	Title
1955	Zhai, Lilin 翟立林	"A Discussion on Architecture as Art in Relation to Aesthetics and National Form," *Architectural Journal* 1955(01) 《論建築藝術與美及民族形式》，《建築學報》1955(01)
1955	Yan, Jiarui 閻家瑞	"Some Comments on Mr. Zhai Lilin's 'A Discussion on the Characteristics of Architecture as Art'," *Architectural Journal* 1955(03) 《對翟立林同志『論建築藝術的特徵』的幾點意見》，《建築學報》1955(03)
1955	Zhou, Xiangyuan 周祥源	"A Discussion on the Content of Architecture as Art – Questioning Mr. Zhai Lilin," *Architectural Journal* 1955(03) 《論建築藝術的內容 — 與翟立林同志商榷》，《建築學報》1955(03)
1956	Chen, Zhihua, Ying, Ruocong 陳志華，英若聰	"A Criticism on Zhai Lilin's 'A Discussion on Architecture as Art in Relation to Aesthetics and National Form'," *Architectural Journal* 1956(02) 《評翟立林『論建築藝術與美及民族形式』》，《建築學報》1956(02)
1957	Zhai, Lilin 翟立林	"Another Discussion on Architecture as Art in Relation to Aesthetics and National Form," *Architectural Journal* 1957(01) 《再論建築藝術與美及民族形式》，《建築學報》1957(01)
1957	Yuan, Zude 袁祖德	"Concerning the Discussion about 'A Discussion on Architecture as Art in Relation to Aesthetics and National Form' – My Views that Differ From Those of Mr. Chen and Mr. Ying," *Architectural Journal* 1957(01) 《在論『建築藝術與美及民族形式』討論中和陳、英兩先生的不同意見》，《建築學報》1957(01)
1954	Zhang, Bo 張鎛	"A Certain Hotel in the Western Suburbs of Beijing," *Architectural Journal* 1954(01) 《北京西郊某招待所設計介紹》，《建築學報》1954(01)
1955	Fan, Rongkang 范榮康	"The Extravagant Yet Impractical Hotel in the Western Suburbs," *Architectural Journal* 1955(01) 《華而不實的西郊招待所》，《建築學報》1955(01)
1960	Theatre Design Group, Tsinghua University 清華大學建築系劇院設計組	"An Introduction of the Design Scheme of the Grand Theater," *Architectural Journal* 1960(05) 《大劇院設計方案介紹》，《建築學報》1960(05)
1957	Zhang, Bo 張鎛	"Qianmen Hotel," *Architectural Journal* 1957(01) 《前門飯店》，《建築學報》1957(01)
1957	Zhou, Buyi 周卜頤	"A Discussion on the Architectural Design of our Country through the Analysis of Several New Buildings in Beijing," *Architectural Journal* 1957(03) 《從北京幾座新建築的分析談我國的建築創作》，《建築學報》1957(03)

1957	Ye, Zugui and Ye, Yaofu 葉祖貴，葉耀富	"Comments on the Design of Qianmen Hotel and a Discussion with Mr. Zhang Bo," *Architectural Journal* 1957(04) 《對前門飯店設計的幾點意見與張鎛先生商榷》，《建築學報》1957(04)
1957	Zhang, Bo 張鎛	"Comments on Commentaries on Qianmen Hotel and a Further Explanation of the Design," *Architectural Journal* 1957(06) 《對前門飯店設計評論的意見和補充說明》，《建築學報》1957(06)
1954		"People Ask Architects to Criticize and Self-Criticize,"*Architectural Journal* 1954(02) 《人們要求建築師展開批評和自我批評》，《建築學報》1954(02)
1996	Wu, Tingli, Zhang, Xiuguo 吳亭莉，張秀國	"Guo'an Theater – a Theater that is Functional, Economical, Novel, Elegant," *Architectural Journal* 1996(05) 《國安劇院 — 一座適用、經濟、新穎、大方的劇場》，《建築學報》1996(05)
1979	Museums and Exhibition Halls Research Group, Tsinghua University 清華大學建工系博覽建築研究小組	"Architectural Designs of Foreign Exhibition Halls and Museums," *Architectural Journal* 1979(02) 《國外展覽館、博物館的建築設計》，《建築學報》1979(02)
1981	Zhang, Depei, Shou, Zhenhua 張德沛，壽震華	"SOM's Works and its Method of Work," *World Architecture* 1981(06) 《SOM 事務所的作品及其工作方法》，《世界建築》1981(06)
2008	Zhou, Qinglin 周慶琳	"A Dream Realized, on National Grand Theater," *Architectural Journal* 2008(01) 《夢想實現 — 記國家大劇院》，《建築學報》2008(01)
2005	Yim, Rocco 嚴迅奇	"Mandarin Palace: a Different Villa Typology," *Time + Architecture* 2005(06) 《九間堂 — 另類的別墅文化》，《時代建築》2005(06)
2008	NA Reporter 新建築記者	"Plainness and Overstatement – Interview with Architect Huang Jie of Qintai Grand Theater," *New Architecture* 2008(02) 《平實與張揚 — 武漢琴台大劇院建築師黃捷訪談》，《新建築》2008(02)
1981	Ying, Ruo 應若	"A Discussion on the Slogan 'Socialist Content, National Form' in Architecture," *Architectural Journal* 1981(02) 《談建築中『社會主義內容，民族形式』的口號》，《建築學報》1981(02)
1981	Wang, Dihua 汪滌華	"Comments on 'A Discussion on the Slogan 'Socialist Content, National Form' in Architecture," *Architectural Journal* 1981(12) 《對『談建築中 '社會主義內容，民族形式' 的口號』的意見》，《建築學報》1981(12)
1983	Editorial Board of Huazhong Architecture 《華中建築》編輯部	"Construct More New Socialist Architecture with Chinese Characteristics," *Huazhong Architecture* 1983(01) 《建設更多具有中國特色的社會主義新型建築》，《華中建築》1983(01)
1981	Wang, Tianxi 王天錫	"An Analysis of the Impact of the Fragrant Hill Hotel Design on Nationalization of China's Architectural Design,'" *Architectural Journal* 1981(06) 《香山飯店設計對中國建築創作民族化的探討》，《建築學報》1981(06)

1983	Gu, Mengchao 顧孟潮	"An Analysis of I.M. Pei's Design Thoughts Through Fragrant Hill Hotel," *Architectural Journal* 1983(04) 《從香山飯店探討貝聿銘的設計思想》，《建築學報》1983(04)
1983	Zhou, Buyi 周卜頤	"Discuss the Modernization and Nationalization in our Country's Architectural Design Through Fragrant Hill Hotel," *New Architecture* 1983(01) 《從香山飯店談我國建築創作的現代化與民族化》，《新建築》1983(01)
2005	Zheng, Shiling 鄭時齡	"Practice of Foreign Architects in China and De-centring of Chinese Architects," *Time + Architecture* 2005(01) 《境外建築師在中國的實驗與中國建築師的邊緣化》，《時代建築》2005(01)
2003	He, Qing 河清	"The Architects Should be Strangled? – Questioning the Winning Tender of CCTV New Headquarters," *New Architecture* 2003(05) 《應當絞死建築師？ — 中央電視台新大樓中標建築方案質疑》，《新建築》2003(05)
2003	Zhu, Tao 朱濤	"Great Leap Forward – Reading of Koolhaas's Design of CCTV New Headquarters," *New Architecture* 2003(05) 《大躍進 — 讀解庫哈斯的 CCTV 新總部大樓》，《新建築》2003(05)

BIBLIOGRAPHY 參考書目

Adams, Maurice B. (1907), "Architecture Journalism," *Journal of the Royal Institute of British Architects*, Third series, Vol. XIV, No.9, 1907

Arendt, Hannah (1958), *Human Condition*, University of Chicago Press

Golden-Biddle, Karen and Rao, Hayagreeva (1997), "Breaches in the Boardroom: Organizational Identity and Conflicts of Commitment in a Nonprofit Organization," *Organization Science*, Vol. 8, No. 6, Nov. - Dec., 1997, p. 593-611

Casson, Hugh (1968), "On Architectural Journalism," in *Concerning Architecture: Essays on Architectural Writers and Writing*, presented to Nikolaus Pevsner, ed. Summerson, John, Allen Lane the Penguin Press, p.258-264

Cheng, Xiaoxi (2005), "Research on the Practice and Communication of Contemporary Architecture Criticism in China," Thesis (Ph.D.), Tsinghua University

Crysler, C. Greig (2003), *Writing Spaces: Discourses of Architecture, Urbanism, and the Built Environment*, 1960-2000, Routledge

Davies, Ian (1979), "China: New Economic Policies," *The Australian Journal of Chinese Affairs*, No.2, Jul. 1979, p.43-55

Greco, Claudio (2008), *Beijing: the New City*, Skira

Gwilt, Joseph (1837), *Elements of Architectural Criticism*, London

Habermas, Jürgen (1989), *The Structural Transformation of the Public Sphere: an Inquiry Into a Category of Bourgeois Society*, The MIT Press

Hays, Michael (1984), "Critical Architecture: Between Culture and Form," *Perspecta*, Vol.21, 1984, p.14-29

Jiang, Miaofei (2004), "Architecture Magazines in China," *Time + Architecture*, 2004(02), p.20-26

Li, Lingyan (2007), "The Observation of the Development of Contemporary Chinese Architecture Through Contemporary Chinese Architectural Journals," Thesis (M. Phil.), Tongji University

Liu, Dongmei (2006), "The Research on Contemporary Chinese Architectural Criticism," Thesis (M. Phil.), Hunan University

Liu, Qing (2003), "Between the State and Market: Media Reform and the Change of Public Discourse in Contemporary China," Thesis (Ph.D.), University of Minnesota

Lu, Duanfang (2006), *Remaking Chinese Urban Form: Modernity, Scarcity and Space*, 1949-2005, Routledge

Lynch, Daniel C. (1999), *After the Propaganda State: Media, Politics, and "Thought Work" in Reformed China*, Stanford University Press

Markus, Thomas A. (2002), *Words Between Spaces: Buildings and Language*, Routledge

Rao, Jialin (2008), "Architectural Criticism on the Mass Communication Environment," Thesis (M. Phil.), Nanchang University

Rendell, Jane (2007), "Site-Writing: Enigma and Embellishment," in *Critical Architecture*, ed. Rendell, Jane, Hill, Jonathan, Fraser, Murray, and Dorrian, Mark, Routledge, p.150-162

Richards, J.M. (1968), "Architectural Criticism in the Nineteen-Thirties," *Concerning Architecture: Essays on Architectural Writers and Writing*, Presented to Nikolaus Pevsner, ed. Summerson, John, Allen Lane the Penguin Press, p.252-257

Rowe, G. Peter and Seng, Kuan (2002), *Architectural Encounters with Essence and Form in Modern China*, The MIT Press

Schwarting, Jon Michael (1985), "In Reference to Habermas," in *Architecture, Criticism, Ideology : Symposium on Architecture and Ideology: Revised Papers*, ed. Ockman, Joan, Princeton Architectural Press

Sennet, Richard (1986), *Fall of Public Man*, Faber

Xue, Charlie Q.L. (2006), *Building a Revolution: Chinese Architecture Since 1980*, Hong Kong University Press

Yang, Yongsheng (2000), Jian zhu bai jia ping lun ji, Beijing : Zhongguo jian zhu gong ye chu ban she

Zeng, Zhaofen (1989), Chuang zuo yu xing shi: dang dai Zhongguo jian zhu ping lun, Tianjin : Tianjin ke xue ji shu chu ban she

Zhu, Jianfei (1998), "Beyond Revolution: Notes on Contemporary Chinese Architecture," *AA files*, Vol. 35, 1998, p.3-14

Zhu, Jianfei (2009), *Architecture of Modern China: a Historical Critique*, Routledge

WEBIBLIOGRAPHY 參考網站

http://www.abbs.com.cn/

http://far2000.com/

http://blog.sina.com.cn/zhutaoarchitect

Dongziba, comment made on 2009-2-23 20:11:59, http://www.wyzxsx.com/Article/Class12/200902/69531.html; consulted on 26 July 2010.

Martinsen, Joel, "Rem Koolhaas and CCTV architecture porn," http://www.danwei.org/architecture/rem_koolhaas_and_cctv_porn.php; consulted on 26 July 2010.

Pei Cobb Freed & Partners, http://www.pcfandp.com/a/p/7905/s.html; consulted on 23 August 2010.